Presented to

_____

From

_____

Date

_____

_____

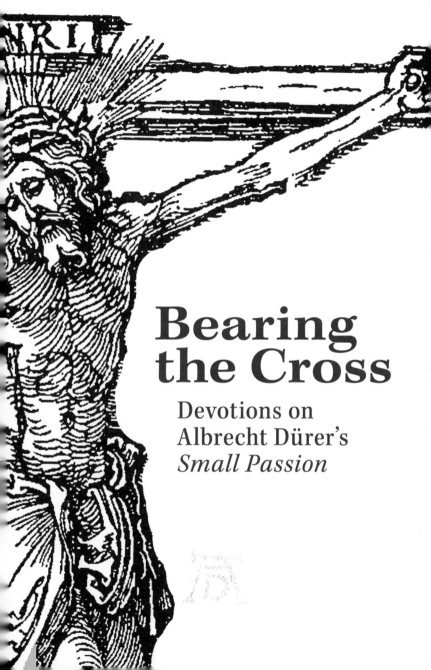

Bearing the Cross

Devotions on
Albrecht Dürer's
Small Passion

Dedicated to my Grandchildren

Claudia Skye

Amelia Raine

Jack Jonathan

Isak Jeremy

Levi Jonathan

and

All the little ones still to come.

Peace and joy in the forgiveness of all your sins on Calvary's cross.

The Lord Jesus be with you, dear children.

Bearing the Cross

Devotions on
Albrecht Dürer's
Small Passion

Carolyn S. Brinkley

CONCORDIA PUBLISHING HOUSE · SAINT LOUIS

Published by Concordia Publishing House

3558 S. Jefferson Ave., St. Louis, MO 63118-3968

1-800-325-3040 • www.cph.org

Manufactured in the United States of America

Library of Congress Cataloging-in-Publication Data

Brinkley, Carolyn S.

  Bearing the cross : devotions on Albrecht Dürer's Small passion / Carolyn S. Brinkley.

    p. cm.

  ISBN 978-0-7586-3140-4

1. Jesus Christ--Passion--Meditations. 2. Dürer, Albrecht, 1471-1528. Kleine Passion. I. Title.

  BT431.3.B75 2012

  232.96--dc23

                          2011041781a

---

1 2 3 4 5 6 7 8 9 10   21 20 19 18 17 16 15 14 13 12

Foreword

By the time Luther gave his "Here I stand" speech at
Worms in the spring of 1521, Albrecht Dürer, the greatest
of the German masters, was firmly in the Lutheran camp.
Shortly thereafter, unaware that the prince of Saxony,
Frederick the Wise, had feigned Luther's kidnapping,
the great artist wrote in his diary that Luther "had been
perfidiously captured;" he feared that Luther would be
murdered.[1]

While Luther spent most of 1521 in hiding at Wartburg
Castle, translating the New Testament into German, his
compatriots in Wittenberg, particularly Andreas Karlstadt
and his band of followers, attacked St. Mary's Church and
denuded it of its "idolatry." Compelled to return, Luther
chastised the people for this act. Worship of images is
idolatry, he preached, but crucifixes, statuary, and paintings
are by no means sinful in and of themselves. In a weeklong
series of sermons begun on Invocavit Sunday, Luther
calmed the situation. To this day, Old St. Mary's Church in
Wittenberg bears the damage inflicted upon its statuary
and images. But Luther repeatedly advocated the proper use
of Christian art—especially and including the crucifix—as
a means for depicting the Word of God and for providing
admonition and consolation for the believer. Wherever the
Lutheran Reformation flourished, so did art. By 1600, there
was more art in city churches in Berlin than before the
Reformation![2]

In 1522 Dürer openly confessed his support for the
Lutheran Reformation—no small thing given the heady
company the artist had kept in his life, having rendered
images of the emperor, his princes, and his scholars. When

Luther's co-reformer, Philip Melanchthon, resided in Nüremberg from 1525 to 26, the artist engraved his portrait as well, sealing a lasting friendship. Though Dürer died unexpectedly on April 6, 1528, at age 57, ten years later his widow, Agnes, transferred an income-producing investment to a foundation in Wittenberg to assist students.

Dürer knew Christ, and suffering. His mother bore eighteen children, and all but two siblings died before him. The artist's life of access and privilege was at every turn tempered by sorrow, death, and loss, and it drove him to Christ. The images of the *Small Passion*—from the fall of Adam and Eve through the stations of the cross, the resurrection, the ascension, and the last judgment—are the artistry of a deep faith already well established prior to Luther's own recovery of the Gospel. As we commemorate the five-hundredth anniversary of the *Small Passion*, there is no question why the series, though only one aspect of the great master's work over a lifetime of achievements in perspective, watercolor landscapes, animal and insect studies, portraits, and altar pieces, has remained his most enduring and popular creation. Beginning with the cover piece, a self-portrait known as *Man of Sorrows*, Dürer is able to meld himself into the suffering of Christ.[3]

The Gospel is not a matter of coercion and force. It's a matter of consolation and pastoral care. Dürer must have rejoiced to the very depths of his anguished being to read Luther for the first time with the conviction that the Gospel of grace is true. I marvel that the great artist could take the woodcut, the oldest form of relief printing, first used in ancient China, to such an amazingly detailed and expressive level. Of all his works, the depiction of death on the face of Christ removed from the cross as the women weep and kiss His crucified feet has always been, for me, the most moving image.

Deaconess Brinkley has given us a wonderful gift. Her meditations on each woodcut explain the detail that a casual or even an interested onlooker would miss—in fact, would never see without her able assistance. How wonderful that the deaconess employs her *diakonia* in leading us more profoundly into the Passion of Christ, as an aid to the great Dürer. What joy is mine that Carolyn is now, through this book, the gift to many that she has already been to my family and me in a special way.

Matthew C. Harrison
The Martyrdom of St. John the Baptist, AD 2011
St. Louis, Missouri

1. Peter Moser, *Albrecht Dürer: His Life, His World and His Art* (Bamberg: Badenber Verlag, 2005), 213.
2. See Bodo Nischan, *Prince, People, and Confession: The Second Reformation in Brandenburg* (Philadelphia: University of Pennsylvania Press, 1994). See especially p. 147.
3. Moser, *Albrecht Dürer*, 221.

Self-Portrait in a Fur-Collared Robe, 1500
Alte Pinakothek, Munich

Albrecht Dürer

Albrecht Dürer (1471–1528) is said to be the greatest German artist of the Northern Renaissance. His works include woodcuts, engravings, sketches, and paintings in both oils and watercolors. Born into a Nuremburg family of goldsmiths, he learned the art of engraving at an early age. Longing to paint, the young Dürer traveled to Italy where he became acquainted with the classical philosophy and techniques of the Southern Renaissance. After some years he returned home to set up his workshop in Nuremburg. With the aid of the newly invented printing press, he became famous throughout Germany for his woodcuts and engravings. As with Luther, available and inexpensive copies of his work propelled Dürer into the public eye. For the first time in history, common people could afford to have artwork in their homes. Dürer became a household name and has remained so in German lands to this very day.

Although Dürer remained a Roman Catholic throughout his life, he became a faithful follower of Luther's teaching. Well-known for his portraits of the wealthy and intellectual, including Frederick the Wise, Emperor Charles V, Melanchthon, and Erasmus, in 1520 he wrote a letter to George Spalatin, secretary to Frederick the Wise, Elector of Saxony: "If God helps me to see Dr. Martin Luther, I shall diligently make his portrait and engrave it as a lasting memory of the Christian man who has helped me out of great anxieties."[1]

---

1. Lewis W. Spitz, *The Renaissance and Reformation Movements* (St. Louis: Concordia, 1971), 326.

Dürer's genius in printmaking forever changed the world of art. Up until this time woodcuts had been merely combinations of black and white. His crosshatching technique proved innovative, bringing new shades of grays to a palette of contrasting light and dark. This greatly enhanced the woodcuts of his *Small Passion*, giving visual depth, dimension, and drama to the biblical narratives.

Besides being a prolific artist in both the religious and secular realms, Dürer was a writer as well. He felt a keen responsibility to pass on his knowledge so that future generations could build on his accomplishments. He developed several illustrated instructional guidebooks on a variety of topics such as mathematics, theoretical and scientific aspects of art, and even military matters and city fortifications in the event of war.

Dürer's last great work in oils was a diptych, or a two-paneled painting, known as *The Four Apostles* or *The Four Holy Men*. This religious scene was completed in 1526, just nine years after the Reformation, and reveals Dürer's newfound faith. It is considered by many as a memorial to his devotion to the Lutheran teachings. The four figures— Saints John, Peter, Paul and Mark—are depicted as real men with no halos. John the Evangelist, a favorite of Luther, looms large in the foreground of the left panel, holding an open New Testament from which he is reading the first verses of his Gospel. Overshadowed by John, and relegated to the background, is the figure of Peter holding the key to heaven. His head is bowed as if in submission to the Word of God being held in front of him. It is significant that Peter is pushed to the background. In traditional Roman Catholic images, Peter is honored as the first pope and founder of the Church and was usually portrayed in places of prominence.

Because he depicted Peter this way, many art historians view Dürer's choice as supporting the Reformation's challenge toward papal authority.

On the right panel is pictured St. Paul, holding a closed Bible and leaning on a sword—a reference to his subsequent execution. Paul's words were influential in Luther's theological development. Behind Paul, nearly blocked from view, is St. Mark, recognized by the scroll in his hand that bears the name of his Gospel. Despite being an evangelist, Mark's turned head and eyes look to Paul as the focal point of the panel. In this profound work Dürer combines visual art with the written word. Attached to the bottom of the paintings the artist leaves a confession of faith in the form of a short essay. "All worldly rulers in this threatening time, beware not to take human delusion for the Word of God. For God wishes nothing added to His Word, nor taken from it. Take to heart therefore the warning of these four excellent men, Peter, John, Paul, and Mark." Dürer added to this selected verses from Martin Luther's 1522 German translation of the Bible: beneath Mark is John's admonition to test the spirits (1 John 4:1–3), and words from Paul about the abuses that will mark the last days (2 Timothy 3:1–7). Beneath the apostle Paul are Jesus' words of warning from Mark's Gospel (Mark 12:38–40) and Peter's warning against destructive heresies (2 Peter 2:1–3). Dürer gave this diptych to the council of Nuremburg to be displayed in the city's secular governmental building. Today it hangs in Munich's Alte Pinakothek art museum as a lasting legacy to this great artist and man of faith.

Introduction

Have you ever wished you could kneel with the shepherds at the manger in Bethlehem? Do you long to stand beneath Calvary's cross? Would you like to walk the Emmaus road and have Easter supper with the risen Lord? *Bearing the Cross* offers this unique devotional opportunity for individual and family worship. Through the exquisite artwork of Albrecht Dürer's *Small Passion* the viewer is invited to become an integral part of the biblical story of salvation. Originally published in 1511, six years before the Reformation, the thirty-seven prints were bound in a pocket devotional containing medieval religious poetry. *Bearing the Cross* takes a fresh look at the woodcuts in light of the doctrine of justification, with the Word of God as the foundation, while poetry from the church's great treasury of hymns enriches each devotional vignette. Although the *Small Passion* is five hundred years old, it remains powerful and compelling; the Dürer prints give the postmodern world a poignant pictorial account spanning mankind's fall in the Garden of Eden, the death of Christ on Calvary's cross, the resurrection, and the last judgment.

During the course of his lifetime, Dürer completed five Passions of Christ. Each series was unique in length and media. The *Small Passion* contains the largest number of scenes, but is known as "small" due to the 4 x 6-inch size of the intricate woodcuts. The pocket-size volume was used for daily devotions by common people.

In addition to being a skilled artist, Dürer was also knowledgeable in Holy Scripture, iconography, and the teachings of the Church of the Middle Ages. Each woodcut of the *Small Passion* comprises a visual sermon that

captures the action and emotion of the entire biblical
account, though three motifs permeated the entirety of the
Small Passion. First, Christ and His work of redemption for
sinful mankind act as the heart and center. Second, Dürer
places himself into the entire work; the distinctive "A. D."
monogram gives him a timely presence, as does the use of
his self-portrait for the face of Adam and also Christ. And
third, he gives the onlooker a unique perspective. It is as if
you are present with Jesus, witnessing His birth, suffering,
death, resurrection, ascension, and final coming.

Bearing the Cross combines the great artwork of
Albrecht Dürer's *Small Passion,* gems of hymnody, and Holy
Scripture into faith-enriching devotional vignettes. The
reader is escorted from Genesis to Revelation on a personal,
intimate journey with Christ.

> What mercy God showed to our race,
> A plan of rescue by His grace:
> In sending One from woman's seed,
> The One to fill our greatest need—
> For on a tree uplifted high
> His only Son for sin would die,
> Would drink the cup of scorn and dread
> To crush the ancient serpent's head!
> (*LSB* 561:3)

Acknowledgements

Bearing the Cross is an unexpected blessing that flowed from my years as a deaconess student at Concordia Theological Seminary, Fort Wayne, Indiana. It began as a final paper in Renaissance and Reformation with Dr. Cameron MacKenzie, and was further nurtured by Prof. Robert Roethemeyer and Dr. Arthur Just, director of the deaconess program. I am very thankful for their help and encouragement, and am also grateful to all the professors at the seminary for the rich theological education I received.

Thank you, President Matthew Harrison, for writing the Foreword. I am deeply honored!

Thank you to Concordia Publishing House, Peter Frank, and all who worked on the publication of the book. Special thanks to Rev. Paul McCain for his kindness and vision.

I'm grateful to my pastor, Rev. William Brege, for his critique, proof-reading, and encouragement.

Many thanks to my supportive family: sons-in-law Rev. Randy Blankschaen and Rev. Jeremy Swem for their consultation and Greek expertise, and the overall enthusiasm from all of my children and their spouses.

Special appreciation goes to my husband, Richard, for his patient listening, suggestions, and knowledge of formatting.

> Bless the Lord, O my soul, and all that is within me, bless His holy name! Bless the Lord, O my soul, and forget not all His benefits. (Psalm 103:1–2)

Carolyn S. Brinkley
Commemoration of St. Barnabas, Apostle

Man of Sorrows

Man of Sorrows

I will put enmity between you and the
woman, and between your offspring
and her offspring; He shall bruise your
head, and you shall bruise His heel.

—Genesis 3:15

The title page of Albrecht Dürer's *Small Passion*
shows Jesus as the Savior of the world. This
illustration encompasses not only His Passion,
but also who Christ is and His work in God's
plan of salvation for fallen mankind. It clearly pictures
the Incarnation, God as man in Jesus of Nazareth. It is the
fulfillment of God's first promise to Adam and Eve in the
Garden of Eden after sin entered the world.

The cruciform halo (also known as a nimbus) depicts
His divine nature, and the unique three pronged rays
represent the Trinity. Yet Christ's human nature is also
portrayed as the Suffering Servant of Isaiah 53, stripped
of the dignity of clothing. He wears the crown of thorns,
unable to hold up His head under the burden of the
world's sin and guilt. His feet, marked with nail prints,
rest on the earth's turf. Even His crucifixion can be seen,
for Jesus' upper body completes the lower portion of the
cross.

But the triumph of Easter is already seen as Christ
sits on the rock of the tomb. "He is not here, but has risen"
(Luke 24:6). His position on the earth brings to mind the
Christmas message of the angels in Luke 2:14: "Glory to God

in the highest, and on earth peace among those with whom He is pleased!"

> Surely He has borne our griefs and carried our sorrows; yet we esteemed Him stricken, smitten by God, and afflicted. (Isaiah 53:4)

> But God shows His love for us in that while we were still sinners, Christ died for us. (Romans 5:8)

God's love to Adam and Eve was immediate after their fall into sin. Although they had abandoned their Creator, God did not abandon His creatures. In Genesis 3:15 the Gospel had already been proclaimed as a promise to Adam and Eve and a curse for Satan. Though the tempter would be defeated, the price would be high. It required perfection and a life of obedience to God that Adam and Eve had exchanged for Satan's lies. They had traded their relationship with God for death. There was nothing they could do to save themselves from eternal separation from their Creator.

This is the condition into which we are all born and in which we all live. We all sin and fall short of the requirements of God's Holy Law. Left to ourselves, we have only death and an eternity in hell. But God, in mercy to His fallen creation, promised to send a Second Adam to be a perfect, sinless, obedient man. This man would be tempted by Satan and yet remain steadfast to the Word of God. He would do battle with Satan and be victorious. Instead of taking out His wrath for our sin on us, the Father places our judgment on Jesus, abandoning His own Son to death on a cross. This Offspring of the woman would take the sin of the world into His own body and defeat Satan by His suffering, death, and resurrection. Jesus would die so that we all might receive forgiveness for our sins and the gift of an eternity with Him in heaven. Come, walk with Christ in His Passion.

O love, how deep, how broad, how high,
Beyond all thought and fantasy,
That God, the Son of God, should take
Our mortal form for mortals' sake!

He sent no angel to our race,
Of higher or of lower place,
But wore the robe of human frame,
And to this world Himself He came.

For us by wickedness betrayed,
For us, in crown of thorns arrayed,
He bore the shameful cross and death;
For us He gave His dying breath.

For us He rose from death again;
For us He went on high to reign;
For us He sent His Spirit here
To guide, to strengthen, and to cheer.

All glory to our Lord and God
For love so deep, so high, so broad;
The Trinity whom we adore
Forever and forevermore.
　　　　　　　(*LSB* 544:1–2, 5–7)

Fall of Man

Adam and Eve

Genesis 2:15–3:15

Dürer, in his opening woodcut, depicts the very last moment of a world without sin. The perfection of Adam and Eve can be seen in their immortal, sinless, graceful bodies, and the perfection of the two "become one flesh" (Genesis 2:24). They are encircled within each others' arms, adoring gazes on their faces as their legs almost seem to entwine. They function as one harmonious unit. Perfect marriage, perfect love, and perfect nakedness stand out in white, starkly contrasted against the foreboding darkness in the background. The tree of knowledge of good and evil is both light and dark, representative of man's free will: obey God, or obey Satan?

In her willingness to hold the forbidden fruit, the serpent and Eve form a unit. Adam does not raise a hand to stop Eve from death, but rather has an open hand ready to receive the fruit, a participant in their catastrophic disobedience. The headship he had been given by God is forgotten as together they abandon their Creator and give allegiance to Satan and themselves.

The animals watch as the perfection of all creation dissolves. Hidden in the shadows of the tree, "the devil prowls around like a roaring lion, seeking someone to devour" (1 Peter 5:8), and the sly-eyed boar, symbol of filth and lust for power, sniffs its prey in eager anticipation. But God does not abandon His creatures! The sacrifice of Christ is already present in the icon of the white ox. The symbol of the white ox has been used since the first century of Christendom to represent the Redeemer who gives His life to ransom mankind. The Second Adam is the promise of a

23

Savior who would be a perfect, sinless man, obedient to God the Father, who would restore perfection by payment for sin on the tree of the cross.

> Therefore, as one trespass led to condemnation for all men, so one act of righteousness leads to justification and life for all men. For as by the one man's disobedience the many were made sinners, so by the one man's obedience the many will be made righteous. (Romans 5:18–19)

Adam takes in his hand the forbidden fruit, and all creation is shaken to its foundation. The one created by God in His image of perfection has transgressed the clear command of his Creator. The change that follows leads us all to destruction. We are the sons and daughters of Adam and carry in us that curse brought about by Adam's sin. We all seek our own way without regard for God or for one another. It is our very nature. Our grave opens before us, and beyond it is an eternity forsaken by God. What can possibly rescue us from this awful misery in which we find ourselves? Who will fight for us, intercede for us, and remove from us the curse of Adam?

Yes, it is all true. We stand before God in the utter nakedness of our own dreadful misdeeds. However, our heavenly Father is a God of boundless grace and mercy, and in His great wisdom He planned our rescue. A Second Adam comes forth, born of a woman and under the Law. Christ leads for us the life we cannot lead for ourselves and then places Himself as the sacrificial Lamb, hung on a cross and forsaken by God in our place. In the Son's act of obedience, the disobedience of Adam and all his sons and daughters is wiped away. "So if the Son sets you free, you will be free indeed" (John 8:36).

> The tree of life with ev'ry good
> In Eden's holy orchard stood,
> And of its fruit so pure and sweet
> God let the man and woman eat.
> Yet in this garden also grew
> Another tree, of which they knew;
> Its lovely limbs with fruit adorned
> Against whose eating God had warned.
>
> The stillness of that sacred grove
> Was broken, as the serpent strove
> With tempting voice Eve to beguile
> And Adam too by sin defile.
> O day of sadness when the breath
> Of fear and darkness, doubt and death,
> Its awful poison first displayed
> Within the world so newly made.
>
> What mercy God showed to our race,
> A plan of rescue by His grace:
> In sending One from woman's seed,
> The One to fill our greatest need—
> For on a tree uplifted high
> His only Son for sin would die,
> Would drink the cup of scorn and dread
> To crush the ancient serpent's head!
> *(LSB* 561:1–3)

Expulsion from Paradise

Expulsion from the Garden

Genesis 3:16–24

The tree of knowledge of good and evil looms large and center in this woodcut. Creation was forever changed by mankind's fall into sin. The top of the tree cannot be seen, for the effects of sin experienced by each generation leads to greater heights of wickedness. The perfect marriage in the previous woodcut now portrays the curse. Adam and Eve are still side-by-side, but no longer in perfect oneness. Rather than legs lovingly entwined, Adam steps on Eve's toes while she stomps on his foot. The struggle between the two sexes will plague mankind until the end of time. As they look back longingly, the face of Adam is clearly seen. It is the same face Dürer uses later in the *Small Passion* for Christ, the Second Adam. Interestingly, it is also the face of Albrecht Dürer in his self-portrait. Is this the face of all humanity made perfect in the Son of Man?

Still the Gospel is yet depicted with Law in this print, for both are within the hands of the angel. The right hand wields the sword that drives Adam and Eve from the beautiful garden they had ruined by their sin. But in God's compassion, the left hand touches Adam gently, but firmly, urging them to flee quickly, thus protecting them from the tree of life, which, if eaten, would eternally trap mankind in death as the consequence of sin.

Therefore, the Lord God sent him out from the Garden of Eden to work the ground from which he was taken. He drove out the man, and at the east of the Garden of Eden he placed the cherubim and a flaming sword that turned every way to guard the way to the tree of life (Genesis 3:23–24).

Adam and Eve were banished from the Garden of Eden. They destroyed their perfect relationship with their Creator when they disobeyed the First Commandment, and the tree designed to show the beautiful fruit of obedience to God became a curse to them. Every aspect of life was perverted by sin. Their perfect marriage was no longer a delight, but filled with conflict. Bearing and raising children was painful. Tending the earth for daily food was backbreaking. No amount of work could undo the curse of death. But in His love God provided a way out. By compelling His fallen creatures to flee the garden, He protected them from eating of the tree of life that would have condemned humanity to an eternity of death.

We are the children of Adam and Eve. We are caught in the inherited sin of our first parents, and pile up evil deeds of our own choosing. Relationships are often troubled. Making ends meet is a constant struggle. No amount of good works will save us from eternal damnation. We have no hope of regaining paradise. But God promised a Savior who did the work for all mankind in another garden. In Gethsemane, the obedient Son triumphed over Satan's temptations and journeyed to Calvary in our place. In the cross of Christ we find anew the tree of life.

> In Adam we have all been one,
>   One huge rebellious man;
> We all have fled that evening voice
>   That sought us as we ran.
>
> We fled Thee, and in losing Thee
>   We lost our brother too;
> Each singly sought and claimed his own;
>   Each man his brother slew.
>
> But Thy strong love, it sought us still
>   And sent Thine only Son
> That we might hear His Shepherd's voice
>   And, hearing Him, be one.
>
> Then shall our song united rise
>   To Thine eternal throne,
> Where with the Father evermore
>   And Spirit Thou art one.
>   (*LSB* 569:1–3, 6)

Annunciation

THE ANNUNCIATION

Luke 1:26–38

Dürer's Passion narrative goes immediately from the fall of mankind in Genesis to the fulfillment of the promise in the New Testament. Gabriel announces to Mary that she has been chosen to be the mother of Jesus, the Son of God. The work of the Holy Trinity is plainly seen as God the Father in the clouds of heaven sends the Holy Spirit in the form of a dove. Mary is pictured devoutly reading Old Testament Scripture, beseeching God to fulfill His promise for a Savior, her hands folded in prayer. The startled Virgin kneels in submission at the angel's stunning words. Her face is sweet, filled with humble joy and awe. The dove hovering over Mary encircles her head with heavenly beams. Gabriel, one hand held out in blessing, the other holding back the curtain, exposes the bed cushion to the radiant light. This conception would occur by the power of the Holy Spirit, for "the Lord Himself will give you a sign. Behold, the virgin shall conceive and bear a Son, and shall call His name Immanuel" (Isaiah 7:14). This Child would be true God and true Man, the perfect Second Adam.

The small plant in the foreground is a reminder of two trees. The first goes back to the Garden of Eden, the tree that brought sin and death into the world. The second is the tree of the cross. It would bring forgiveness and life to mankind by another's death.

> And behold, you will conceive in your womb and bear a son, and you shall call His name Jesus. He will be great and will be called the Son of the Most High. And the Lord God will give to Him the throne of His father David, and He will reign over the house of Jacob forever, and of His kingdom there will be no end. (Luke 1:31–33)

God's faithful people had been waiting for thousands of years. When would He fulfill His promise? Who would come to undo the great evil that began in the Garden of Eden? In God's perfect timing, He sent the angel Gabriel to a small village in Galilee with a stunning message for Mary, a young, unmarried girl. All the prophecies of the Old Testament would be accomplished through her, in her, and for her, and thus for all mankind. It would be a miracle! The virgin would conceive by the power of the Holy Spirit, and give birth to the long awaited Savior. His name would be Jesus. He would save His people from their sins by accomplishing the greatest work since creation. This human baby would be nothing less than the true God Himself! He would be a descendant of King David and rule as king over the new creation. He would bestow gifts of forgiveness, life, and salvation. His kingdom would be eternal. What astonishing news!

How did Mary respond? "Behold, I am the servant of the Lord; let it be to me according to Your word" (Luke 1:38a). What an amazing confession of faith! Mary humbly, obediently, and joyfully submitted her heart and body to the service of the Lord. What a beautiful confession of faith for every woman, man, and child to emulate! So grant us, heavenly Father.

Savior of the nations, come,
Virgin's Son, make here Your home!
Marvel now, O heav'n and earth,
That the Lord chose such a birth.

Not by human flesh and blood,
By the Spirit of our God,
Was the Word of God made flesh—
Woman's offspring, pure and fresh.

Here a maid was found with child,
Yet remained a virgin mild.
In her womb this truth was shown:
God was there upon His throne.

Then stepped forth the Lord of all
From His pure and kingly hall;
God of God, yet fully man,
His heroic course began.

Glory to the Father sing.
Glory to the Son, our king,
Glory to the Spirit be
Now and through eternity.
                    (*LSB* 332:1–4, 8)

Nativity

THE NATIVITY

Luke 2:1–21

Dürer stations the viewer on the lowest level of the stable, which provides a delightful intimacy for this charming depiction of the Christmas story. Contemporary man is invited to kneel in worship with the Renaissance shepherds and become part of the Lukan account. The stable, in appalling condition, signifies our Lord's state of humiliation "who for us men and for our salvation came down from heaven" (Nicene Creed). But the stable is also elevated to honor the newborn King. Mary's hands are clasped over her heart in wonder and prayer as she bows in reverence to her son and Savior. Joseph, the earthly father, is seen on the edge of the woodcut. His gaze is intense and watchful, and he provides light for the little one entrusted to his care.

The heart and center of the scene is the sweet Christ Child in a basket, attended by a tiny angel. The baby Jesus has outstretched arms, suggestive of the way He would one day stretch out His arms on the cross. The cross, alluded to by the sprig in the *Annunciation* woodcut, peaks out beneath the rugged cross piece of the stable roof.

The artist has simultaneously portrayed all elements of the nativity narrative. In the background the angel brings "good news of great joy" to shepherds tending sheep on the hillside (Luke 2:10). The entire illustration is bathed in the twinkling light of the morning star, reminding the viewer of those who will bow in homage to the light of the world.

> And the angel said to them, "Fear not, for behold, I bring you good news of great joy that will be for all the people. For unto you is born this day in the city of David a Savior, who is Christ the Lord. And this will be a sign for you: you will find a baby wrapped in swaddling cloths and lying in a manger." (Luke 2:10–12)

The time had come for God to redeem His people. These verses are some of the most beloved and well-known in all Scripture. We've heard them many times, but each and every time we hear the account of the birth of Christ, our Lord has new and deeper things to reveal to us about His great love. These passages are not just a rehash of ancient history. They proclaim the present reality of the incarnation of Christ. God the Creator of all things has permanently joined Himself to His creatures in the flesh and bone of a tiny baby. Such an ordinary newborn wrapped in swaddling clothes, rather like the diapers you and I wore in infancy. So little and so helpless, the Bread of Life lies in an animal feeding trough. Yet this is the very Son of God! He is the Savior who would live the perfect life for us, die our death and rise to life, ushering in the new creation. He came to take all our sin and misery, from the time of Adam and Eve to the grave. It is this Christ Child who gives the true gifts of Christmas—forgiveness, life, and salvation!

O sing of Christ, whose birth made known
    The kindness of the Lord,
Eternal Word made flesh and bone
    So we could be restored.
Upon our frail humanity
    God's finger chose to trace
The fullness of His deity,
    The icon of His grace.

What Adam lost, none could reclaim,
    And Paradise was barred
Until the second Adam came
    To mend what sin had marred.
For when the time was full and right
    God sent His only Son;
He came to us as life and light
    And our redemption won.

Lord Jesus Christ, you deigned to dwell
    Among us here on earth
As God with us, Emmanuel,
    To bring this holy birth.
Though rich, You willingly became
    One with our poverty,
That we might share Your wealth and name
    For all eternity!
               (*LSB* 362:1–2, 4)

Christ Taking Leave of His Mother

THE FAMILY OF JESUS

Luke 2:34–35; 18:31–33; Mark 3:31–35

The woodcuts of the *Small Passion* jump from the Christ's birth to His journey to Jerusalem and the cross. This woodcut is a summary of several texts, rather than an exact incident as recorded in Scripture. It is Jesus' good-bye to His family. Three of the Gospels record that Mary and Jesus' siblings came to find Him during His ministry, no doubt wanting to bring Him home. At that point, Jesus distanced Himself from His birth family in order to include all believers as His family. He must be the obedient Son and give His life on the cross so that all can be children of the heavenly Father.

In the scene illustrated by Dürer, Jesus looks with tender sadness at His mother, knowing that He would view her from the cross, not as just a son but as her Savior. He knew that Mary, with a mother's heart, would experience acute pain at His crucifixion. Mary is seen on bended knee, begging her son to stay home where it is safe. The prophecy of Simeon, spoken over thirty years earlier when her forty-day-old baby was presented at the temple, is a sword, piercing her heart and soul. In the background, Jerusalem waits, and behind it rises Mount Calvary. The tree of the cross, depicted in previous woodcuts, is now full grown. The disciples are waiting. It is time to go.

And taking the twelve, He said to them, "See, we are going up to Jerusalem, and everything that is written about the Son of Man by the prophets will be accomplished. For He will be delivered over to the Gentiles and will be mocked and shamefully treated and spit upon. And after flogging Him, they will kill Him, and on the third day He will rise." (Luke 18:31–33)

As Jesus prepares to go to Jerusalem, He tells His disciples exactly what's going to happen. Yet they don't understand. Even though minute details of the Passion had been prophesied in the Old Testament, they don't get it. It doesn't fit with their plans. Who wants a Messiah who is publicly killed as a common criminal? It's distasteful, shameful, and scandalous, even to us today. It doesn't make sense. But that was precisely God's plan. He humbled Himself to take all our punishment for sin into His own body. The Son of God suffered humiliation, degradation, and death in our place in order to restore the family of God, first shattered by Adam and Eve's catastrophic disobedience. He gave His life to heal the broken relationship between God and man. His death freely gives forgiveness, life, and salvation.

But how do these blessings of the cross become ours? How can I be certain that my sins are forgiven? How can I know for sure that I am God's child? How can I know with absolute certainty that I am included in the family of God? In Christ we are made children of the heavenly Father through the waters of Holy Baptism. In Baptism, God puts His holy name on us and claims us as His own dear children, "for in Christ Jesus you are all sons of God, through faith. For as many of you as were baptized into Christ have put on Christ" (Galatians 3:26–27).

> Baptized into Your name most holy,
>   O Father, Son, and Holy Ghost,
> I claim a place, though weak and lowly,
>   Among Your saints, Your chosen host.
> Buried with Christ and dead to sin,
> Your Spirit now shall live within.
>
> My loving Father, here You take me
>   To be henceforth Your child and heir.
> My faithful Savior, here You make me
>   The fruit of all Your sorrows share.
> O Holy Spirit, comfort me
> When threat'ning clouds around I see.
>
> My faithful God, You fail me never;
>   Your promise surely will endure.
> O cast me not away forever
>   If words and deeds become impure.
> Have mercy when I come defiled;
> Forgive, lift up, restore Your child.
>
> All that I am and love most dearly—
>   Receive it all, O Lord, from me.
> Let me confess my faith sincerely;
>   Help me your faithful child to be!
> Let nothing that I have or own
> Serve any will but Yours alone.
>   (*LSB* 590:1–4)

Christ's Entry into Jerusalem

CHRIST'S ENTRY INTO JERUSALEM

Luke 19:28–40

n the Palm Sunday woodcut, Jesus is the sole rider in the procession. As a sign of royalty, His colt is draped with garments. Bethany at Mount Olivet—the home of His close friends Mary, Martha, and Lazarus—can be seen in the distance. Jerusalem, the city where Christ would die in less than a week, looms close. This is the first time the light at Christ's head, known as the trinitarian nimbus, has been seen since Dürer's title page. It is in the form of a cross. The halo is bright, but the face of Christ is dark as He approaches the gate of Jerusalem.

The people are divided into two groups. On the right, His disciples can be seen spreading a cloak in His path, lifting their hands in prayer, waving palm branches in honor of King Jesus, and singing Hosannas to the Son of David. On the left, one of the Pharisees points an accusing finger at the back of Christ, identifying Him as the one they are plotting to kill. In contrast, Jesus lifts His hand in peace and blessing. The viewer is given a strategic position alongside Jesus as He enters the city gate. The Son of God and the Son of Man obediently and willingly rides to His death. Will you enter Jerusalem with Christ? Will you follow Him to the cross?

> Rejoice greatly, O daughter of Zion! Shout aloud, O daughter of Jerusalem! Behold your king is coming to you; righteous and having salvation is He, humble and mounted on a donkey, on a colt, the foal of a donkey. (Zechariah 9:9)

Jesus knew the religious leaders wanted to kill Him. Their rejection of Him had been mounting throughout His three-year ministry. They had no use for a Messiah who preached repentance, healed the sick, and raised the dead. They looked for an earthly king who would restore the glory and power of Israel. Despite the danger, Christ deliberately entered their territory. Our Lord did not quietly sneak in the back door, but boldly entered Jerusalem, riding on a colt. The royal processional publicly proclaimed Jesus as the fulfillment of Old Testament prophecies. He was God's promised One to redeem Israel. The people were elated! They loved the miracles and found pleasure in celebrating a king who would feed bread to the multitudes.

Just like them, we also crave the glory and pomp of an earthly savior, rather than spiritual riches. We'd much rather stay at the festive Palm Sunday parade than walk the funeral procession to Calvary. But Jesus, the Son of God, was no ordinary king. He came to die. This King came in meekness, burdened with the sin of the world—our sin. His crown would not boast costly gems, but was jeweled with thorns and stained with blood, meant to purchase our crown of life. He rode not to a throne, but to a cross.

Ride on, ride on in majesty!
Hark! All the tribes hosanna cry.
O Savior meek, pursue Thy road,
With palms and scattered garments strowed.

Ride on, ride on in majesty!
In lowly pomp ride on to die.
O Christ, Thy triumphs now begin
O'er captive death and conquered sin.

Ride on, ride on in majesty!
The angel armies of the sky
Look down with sad and wond'ring eyes
To see the approaching sacrifice.

Ride on, ride on in majesty!
Thy last and fiercest strife is nigh.
The Father on His sapphire throne
Awaits His own anointed Son.

Ride on, ride on in majesty!
In lowly pomp ride on to die.
Bow Thy meek head to mortal pain,
Then take, O God, Thy pow'r and reign.
(*LSB* 441:1–5)

*Christ Driving the Money-Changers
from the Temple*

CHRIST DRIVING THE MONEY-CHANGERS FROM THE TEMPLE

Mark 11:15–19

his print depicts the chaotic scene in which Jesus cleanses the temple on Monday morning of Holy Week. What was to be a holy place of worship had been turned into an unholy place of market transactions. The image of Christ in His divine wrath dominates the entire woodcut. The stark whiteness of His garment contrasts with His face, dark in anger as He proclaims, "My house shall called a house of prayer, but you make it a den of robbers" (Matthew 21:13). The candle, perched high in the gloom of the temple wall, represents the light of the world. "The light has come into the world, and people loved the darkness rather than the light because their works were evil" (John 3:19).

Dürer incorporates the whip of cords from the account recorded in John 2:13–17 as Christ forcefully overturns the money-changer's table. The banker and his coins spill to the floor. The artist's monogram sits cockeyed in the bottom corner as if it had been knocked from the tumbled bench. Priests and scribes, clutching one another in fear, retreat with new zeal to kill Jesus of Nazareth. As a merchant scurries to escape, he tucks a Passover lamb under his arm while *the* Passover Lamb reveals the righteous anger of God at mankind's disobedience.

> These I will bring to My holy mountain, and make them joyful in My house of prayer; their burnt offerings and their sacrifices will be accepted on My altar; for My house shall be called a house of prayer for all peoples. (Isaiah 56:7)

It was only natural that Jesus, the obedient Son of God, would journey to Jerusalem to observe the Passover. This was part of fulfilling God's Law, which He did even as a child. And the first place He would go in the city would be the temple. This was His Father's house. It was not just a symbolic location, but was the dwelling place of the real presence of God. This was where the Creator chose to dwell on earth with His creatures. But just as in the Garden of Eden, Satan strove to destroy this relationship. Rather than a place of worship for all nations, the temple had been defiled with fraudulent business. The sacrifices, which were intended to remind the Israelites of the great cost of their sin and of God's promised Messiah, had been perverted. God's name was despised. In holy wrath, Christ, the incarnate Son of God, purged the "den of robbers." They had cheated God by dishonoring His holiness. They had rejected God's loving presence.

Are we any different? How often do we reject the real presence of Christ in His Word and Sacraments? How often do we go through the motions of worship, with hearts and minds elsewhere? How often are we more concerned with earthly goods than God's gracious spiritual gifts? We are all in need of a Savior. Jesus, the Passover Lamb of God, was the perfect and final sacrifice for all our sin. In the cross of Christ we stand in the presence of God as His forgiven children.

To Thee, omniscient Lord of all,
In grief and shame I humbly call;
    I see my sins against Thee, Lord,
    The sins of thought and deed and word.
They press me sore; I cry to Thee:
O God, be merciful to me!

O Lord, my God, to Thee I pray:
O cast me not in wrath away!
    Let Thy good Spirit ne'er depart,
    But let Him draw to Thee my heart
That truly penitent I be:
O God, be merciful to me!

O Jesus, let Thy precious blood
Be to my soul a cleansing flood.
    Turn not, O Lord, Thy guest away,
    But grant that justified I may
Go to my house at peace with Thee:
O God, be merciful to me!

              (*LSB* 613:1–3)

Christ Washing the Feet of St. Peter

CHRIST WASHING THE DISCIPLES' FEET

John 13:1–17

On Maundy Thursday evening, Jesus teaches His disciples one last lesson on love before the agony of His punishment begins, in an interlude during the Passover celebration. The image of our Lord is that of a servant. He has removed His outer garment and tied a towel around His waist. Perhaps it is John attending Christ, holding his cloak and water pitcher. Possibly John's brother James is the disciple with his hands clasped in prayer. These two, along with Peter, are Jesus' closest friends. The artist depicts them in the form of a triangle, an arrangement that anticipates their intimate participation at Gethsemane. Having washed the other disciples' feet, it is now Peter's turn. Reluctance in his posture, Peter has one foot in the pan of water while Jesus washes the other. The disciple sits and scratches his head, a perplexed look on his face. The picture is tender and sweet as Jesus, kneeling before His disciples, holds Peter's leg with one hand and scrubs the bottom of his foot with the other.

The artist stations the viewer so close that you feel you are next in line to plunge your feet into the basin. In the background the disciples watch, agitated and confused on hearing their Teacher say, "And you are clean, though not every one of you" (John 13:10). How could this be? All twelve are accounted for by Dürer, though one stands in the darkness just outside the doorway. Could this be Judas? Just minutes earlier Jesus would have washed the feet of Judas.

What great love! The Lord of all stoops to be the servant of all—even His betrayer!

> Now before the Feast of the Passover, when Jesus
> knew that His hour had come to depart out of this
> world to the Father, having loved His own who
> were in the world, He loved them to the end. . . .
> then He poured water into a basin and began to
> wash His disciples' feet and to wipe them with the
> towel that was wrapped around Him. (John 13:1, 5)

The Passover meal was a lengthy celebration, consisting of eating and liturgy. It commemorated God's loving rescue of His people when they were slaves in Egypt. During the course of the evening, Jesus left the feast table to teach His disciples through a real-life visual and sensory object lesson of His love. It summarized His entire ministry. Jesus did many works of kindness. He came to serve. He healed the sick and fed the hungry. Dressed as a slave, Jesus washed His disciples' feet.

But in Christ's greatest work of service, He gave His innocent life in exchange for our sin and guilt. He is the perfect Passover Lamb whose blood cleanses us from all sins. He is our example of how we are to serve and love others. As Christ has forgiven us, we are to forgive others. Forgiveness is our greatest act of service to our neighbor. It is the heart of the Lord's Prayer: "And forgive us our trespasses as we forgive those who trespass against us." This is the summary of the Christian life in which serving one's neighbor in his physical and spiritual need is the vocation of those who follow Christ.

Jesus knew the end of His ministry had come. "Knowing that the Father had given all things into His hands" (John 13:3), He would be betrayed by one of His beloved disciples and abandoned by all. His Passion was only several hours away. He willingly becomes the Servant whose death on the cross would wash away our sins.

Jesus, greatest at the table,
    The almighty Son of Man,
Laid aside His outer clothing,
    Poured some water in a pan;
As the Twelve lay, hushed in silence,
    He the servant's task began.

Marvel how their Lord and teacher
    Gently taught them not to vie
As He humbly knelt before them,
    Dusty feet to wash and dry,
By His tender touch expressing
    True compassion from on high.

Jesus took the role of servant
    When upon that gruesome span,
For all human sin He suffered
    As a vile and loathsome man;
On the cross poured out like water
    To fulfill the Father's plan.

Can we fathom such deep mercy?
    Do we see what God has done?
Who can grasp this great reversal:
    Love that gives His only Son?
Christ, the sinless for the sinners,
    For the many dies the One.
            (*LSB* 446:1–4)

Last Supper

THE LAST SUPPER

John 13:21–30

ürer's *Last Supper* does not focus on Christ's institution of the Lord's Supper itself, but rather portrays the announcement of the betrayal of Judas. In this scene, the Passover meal has been eaten. The plates are empty and a platter in the center of the table contains the remnants of the roasted lamb.

Positioned directly in line with Jesus and the lamb, a drinking cup and half a loaf of unleavened bread allude to the Lord's Supper. A knife is pointed at the hand of Judas. He sits on the edge of the group of disciples, clutching a full moneybag—the thirty pieces of silver for which he betrayed Jesus. Behind Judas stands the water pitcher used just minutes earlier when Christ washed his feet. As Jesus announces the betrayal, the disciples' faces express consternation. John, leaning on Jesus and wrapped in His arm, is downcast in sadness. The eyes of Jesus and Judas meet. "Is it I, Rabbi?" The face of Christ is filled with poignant love and sorrow. "You have said so" (Matthew 26:25).

> Now as they were eating, Jesus took bread, and
> after blessing it broke it and gave it to the disciples,
> and said, "Take, eat; this is my body." And he took
> a cup, and when he had given thanks he gave it
> to them, saying, "Drink of it, all of you, for this is
> my blood of the covenant, which is poured out
> for many for the forgiveness of sins." (Matthew
> 26:26–28)

After Jesus washes the disciples' feet, the Passover
celebration continues, but in a remarkable and new way.
Christ, the final and perfect Passover Lamb, would be
sacrificed in a few short hours. The blood of Christ shed on
Calvary's cross would give forgiveness, life, and salvation to
all believers. His death would bring peace between God and
man. This was what the world has been waiting for since
the Garden of Eden. But how can we receive these gifts?
How can we travel back two thousand years to Calvary?
We can't, so Christ comes to us poor, helpless sinners each
and every time the Lord's Supper is celebrated. He comes
with forgiveness for all believers, in all times and places.
He comes with His true body and true blood in the simple
elements of His creation—bread and wine. How can this
be? How do I know this is true? How do I know these
gifts are for me? We believe because Christ says this. In
the institution of the Lord's Supper, He gives us His word
"poured out for many for the forgiveness of sins" (Matthew
26:28). On the cross He shed His holy precious blood for
you and me. What great love! In the Sacrament of Holy
Communion, our crucified and risen Lord comes to us.

'Twas on that dark, that doleful night
When pow'rs of earth and hell arose
Against the Son of God's delight
And friends betrayed Him to His foes.

Before the mournful scene began,
He took the bread and blessed and brake.
What love thro' all His actions ran!
What wondrous words of grace He spake!

"This is My body, broke for sin;
Receive and eat the living food";
Then took the cup and blessed the wine:
"'Tis the new cov'nant in My Blood."

"Do this," He said, "till time shall end,
In mem'ry of your dying Friend.
Meet at My table and record
The love of your departed Lord."

Jesus, Thy feast we celebrate;
We show Thy death, we sing Thy name,
Till Thou return and we shall eat
The marriage supper of the Lamb.
(*TLH* 164:1–5)

Agony in the Garden

AGONY IN THE GARDEN

Matthew 26:36–46; Luke 22:39–46

The Passion agony of our Savior's suffering begins in earnest in the Garden of Gethsemane. It brings back memories of the Garden of Eden and the sin of the first Adam's disobedience. The image of Christ, the Second Adam, is the center of the woodcut. He is the entire center of God's plan of salvation. Surrounded by darkness, Jesus is seen in great agony of body and soul. Kneeling in prayer, He begs His heavenly Father to find another way to redeem sinful mankind, but humbly and obediently submits to His Father's will. Even His feet are shown in the tight grip of fear and dread. Above, in white clouds of glory, an angel descends from heaven, bringing Christ His cross.

Beneath Jesus are the three disciples—His dearest friends. They had witnessed His glory at the transfiguration, but now cannot bear the sight of Christ's humanity, battling with the tempter. Peter slumbers, sword clutched in his hand. Another bows his head in sleep and grief. Although Scripture clearly states that all three slept, Dürer portrays the third disciple yet awake, his upturned face intense as he watches Jesus. Far in the distance, the enemies of Christ can be seen leaving Jerusalem with flaming torches, ready to capture the Son of Man.

And He came out and went, as was His custom,
to the Mount of Olives, and the disciples followed
Him. And when He came to the place, He said
to them, "Pray that you may not enter into
temptation." And He withdrew from them about a
stone's throw, and knelt down and prayed, saying,
"Father, if You are willing, remove this cup from
Me. Nevertheless, not My will, but Yours be done."
(Luke 22:39–42)

After celebrating the Passover, Jesus and His disciples
walked to the Garden of Gethsemane, a grove of olive trees
less than a mile from Jerusalem. It was here in the darkness
of night that Jesus faced the fiercest temptation in mankind's
history. It was a temptation that had grown its gnarled roots
in the Garden of Eden. The Messiah, God's promised rescuer,
the perfect Adam, had come to battle with Satan once and
for all. We see the humanity of Christ as He suffers great
anguish of body and soul, knowing that it is time for Him to
die. As an innocent man, He bears the wrath of God for the
sin of the entire world—from Adam until the end of time.
Jesus is consumed with anxiety and dread. Death and life
are locked in mortal combat. Struggling with the temptation
to turn His back on the cross, Jesus places Himself into His
Father's hands. In His obedience, He crushes Satan's head
for us.

Our Savior knows our terrible internal struggles. We are
like the disciples. Where Jesus the Son of God is victorious in
temptation, we are failures. On our own we have no strength
to survive Satan's cunning. Jesus knows the weakness of our
human flesh and invites us to cry out to Him in the midst of
our temptations. He hears our prayer and strengthens us.

When we fall into sin, He grants us forgiveness through His sacrifice on the tree of the cross.

Go to dark Gethsemane,
All who feel the tempter's pow'r;
Your Redeemer's conflict see,
Watch with Him one bitter hour;
Turn not from His griefs away;
Learn from Jesus Christ to pray.

Follow to the judgment hall,
View the Lord of life arraigned;
Oh, the wormwood and the gall!
Oh, the pangs His soul sustained!
Shun not suff'ring, shame, or loss;
Learn from Him to bear the cross.

Calv'ry's mournful mountain climb;
There, adoring at His feet,
Mark that miracle of time,
God's own sacrifice complete.
"It is finished!" hear Him cry;
Learn from Jesus Christ to die.

Early hasten to the tomb
Where they laid His breathless clay;
All is solitude and gloom.
Who has taken Him away?
Christ is ris'n! He meets our eyes.
Savior, teach us so to rise.

(*LSB* 436:1–4)

Betrayal of Christ

THE BETRAYAL OF CHRIST

Matthew 26:47–56

The chaos of an angry mob with spears, soldiers, and torches reigns over the woodcut of Christ's betrayal in the garden. Though the entirety of the account appears to happen at once, the eye is drawn to two figures, seemingly frozen and oblivious to the violent situation around them. Jesus sees only Judas. He feels only the pain of betrayal. He feels only the arms of His disciple, one of His chosen twelve, as He is wrapped in mock embrace. "Friend," Jesus speaks, giving Judas Iscariot opportunity to repent, "Do what you came to do" (Matthew 26:50). Faces meet in the kiss.

Behind Judas, the tree brings the viewer back to the Garden of Eden. Judas, like Adam, betrays God for his own self-interest.

In the foreground, Peter attempts to defend His Lord. He strikes the servant of the high priest with his sword as the victim falls to the ground, tearing at Peter's clothes and kicking his chest, his lantern his only shield. A riot nearly breaks out, and a soldier begins to pull Judas from Christ. Behind Jesus, the rope is readied to bind the hands of the prisoner. The night of evil has begun.

> Do you think that I cannot appeal to My Father and
> He will at once send Me more than twelve legions
> of angels? But how then should the Scriptures be
> fulfilled, that it must be so? (Matthew 26:53–54)

The account in the Garden of Gethsemane clearly shows the two natures of Christ. He is at once true God and true man. First we see His humanity in His bloody sweat as Jesus dreads His imminent suffering and death. Yet accepting His Father's will, He rises from prayer to place Himself into the hands of those who will kill Him. As He greets the large mob sent by the religious leaders, we see the divine majesty of our Savior. He is in perfect control as the powers of darkness seek to destroy God's plan of salvation by destroying the sinless Son of God. When Satan uses a disciple of Jesus to betray Christ, our Lord responds by giving Judas opportunity for repentance. Then Satan uses a crowd armed with swords and clubs to capture Christ. But it is Jesus who confronts them with His Godhead, saying "I Am He." At once "they drew back and fell to the ground" (John 18:6). Finally, Satan uses the violence of Peter to start a riot. But Jesus heals the victim, restoring peace.

Why? Why does our Lord willingly let Himself be treated as a dangerous criminal, to be falsely arrested and humiliated by the kiss of hypocrisy? He does this for you and for me. He is our perfect substitute. He is the perfect sacrifice that pays the enormous debt of our sin. What comfort this is for the troubled conscience! No matter how hard we try to be perfect in our work, in our relationships with others, and in all aspects of our lives, we end up as failures. So God sent a Savior to be perfect for us. He is true man under the Law, the obedient Second Adam born to die our death. He is true God, died to rise from the grave in order to give us new life. Christ does for us what we cannot do for ourselves. He is the Messiah promised in the Garden of Eden. "But all this has taken place that the Scriptures of the prophets might be fulfilled" (Matthew 26:56a).

> If Your beloved Son, O God,
>   Had not to earth descended
> And in our mortal flesh and blood
>   Had not sin's power ended,
> Then this poor, wretched soul of mine
> In hell eternally would pine
>   Because of my transgression.
>
> But now I find sweet peace and rest;
>   Despair no more reigns o'er me.
> No more am I by sin oppressed,
>   For Christ has borne sin for me.
> Upon the cross for me He died
> That, reconciled, I might abide
>   With You, my God, forever.
>
> All righteousness by works is vain;
>   The Law brings condemnation.
> True righteousness by faith I gain;
>   Christ's work is my salvation.
> His death, that perfect sacrifice,
> Has paid the all sufficient price;
>   In Him my hope is anchored.
>
> My guilt, O Father, You have laid
>   On Christ, Your Son, my Savior.
> Lord Jesus, You my debt have paid
>   And gained for me God's favor.
> O Holy Spirit, Fount of grace,
> The good in me to You I trace;
>   In faith and hope preserve me.
>   (*LSB* 568:1–4)

Christ before Annas

CHRIST BEFORE ANNAS

John 18:12–14, 19–24

Arrested and bound, Jesus begins a series of trials during the night. He is first taken to Annas, a man of great influence and also the former high priest. He is also the father-in-law of Caiaphas, the current high priest and the driving force behind the plot to kill Jesus. After Jesus raised Lazarus from the dead, some time before the beginning of His Passion, Caiaphas had met with the Sanhedrin to plan Jesus' death, arguing that "it is better for you that one Man should die for the people, not that the whole nation should perish" (John 11:50).

Dürer's woodcut shows the fruit their plan has borne, as Jesus' abuse at the hands of the temple officials begins. His hands are tied behind His back. An armed guard pulls Him by the hair, dragging Him up the stairs to be presented to Annas in this private, illegal session. Behind Jesus, the soldier keeps one hand on the rope while the other presses the handle of a dagger into His back. Above all this, a third guard wields a club as he presses Christ downward. Annas watches the degradation of Christ from his throne, a ruler's stick of authority in hand. Next to him stand several priests and scribes. One lays a hand on Annas' shoulder as if to say, "We've got Him now. He'll soon be dead."

So the band of soldiers and their captain and the officers of the Jews arrested Jesus and bound Him. First they led Him to Annas, for he was the father-in-law of Caiaphas, who was high priest that year. It was Caiaphas who had advised the Jews that it would be expedient that one man should die for the people. (John 18:12–14)

Although Caiaphas did not know it, he spoke the truth of God's plan of salvation. Christ, the sinless Son of God, would die to save all people. The prisoner who stood bound before Annas would free mankind from the shackles of the evil one. By His death the captive would release creation from sin, death, and Satan. He was captured so we can live in the freedom of sins forgiven.

Only the Gospel of John records the first trial in our Lord's Passion. After His arrest in the Garden of Gethsemane, Jesus is taken back into Jerusalem to be interrogated by Annas. Though Jewish law stated that trials could not be held before the morning sacrifice, this trial is held deep in the night of Satan's darkness. Here we see our Savior's hands tied with ropes. Here we see the Lord of creation take our bondage of sin on Himself.

Annas questions Jesus—what did He preach? "The Spirit of the Lord is upon Me, because He has anointed Me to proclaim good news to the poor. He has sent Me to proclaim liberty to the captives and recovering of sight to the blind, to set at liberty those who are oppressed" (Luke 4:18). Christ preached that He was the Messiah, the fulfillment of the Scriptures. He was the One who came to release us from the bondage begun in the Garden of Eden by Adam's rebellion.

Enslaved by sin and bound in chains,
Beneath its dreadful tyrant sway,
And doomed to everlasting pains,
We wretched, guilty captives lay.

Nor gold nor gems could buy our peace,
Nor all the world's collected store
Suffice to purchase our release;
A thousand worlds were all too poor.

Jesus, the Lord, the mighty God,
An all sufficient ransom paid.
O matchless price! His precious blood
For vile, rebellious traitors shed.

Jesus the Sacrifice became
To rescue guilty souls from hell;
The spotless, bleeding, dying Lamb
Beneath avenging Justice fell.

Amazing goodness! Love divine!
Oh, may our grateful hearts adore
The matchless grace nor yield to sin
Nor wear its cruel fetters more!

(TLH 141:1–5)

Christ before Caiaphas

CHRIST BEFORE CAIAPHAS

Matthew 26:57–66

nnas sends Jesus to Caiaphas, the high priest. Christ, hands and neck bound with rope, is escorted by armed guards, a cluster of spears behind Him. The official trial takes place before the entire Sanhedrin, composed of seventy-one members. False witnesses testify, but none can agree on a crime. Jesus remains quiet. Finally, Caiaphas, sitting on an elegant, cushioned throne, commands Jesus to speak, hoping to catch Him in blasphemy. "I adjure You by the living God, tell us if You are the Christ, the Son of God" (Matthew 26:63). Assuming Jesus is defying authority by His silence, a soldier moves to strike Him while the other guard points to Caiaphas. Jesus responds, "You have said so" (Matthew 26:64).

This is the dramatic moment that Dürer captures in his woodcut. Upon hearing Jesus proclaim the truth of the high priest's own words, the corpulent Caiaphas pronounces the verdict: blasphemy. He tears his clothes in outrage, but his angry face is gleeful. At last, he finally has grounds for the death penalty! Even the little dog at his feet looks smug. In contrast, the face of our Savior remains somber and resolute. His course to the cross is set.

But Jesus remained silent. And the high priest
said to Him, "I adjure you by the living God, tell
us if You are the Christ, the Son of God." Jesus
said to him, "You have said so. But I tell you, from
now on you will see the Son of Man seated at the
right hand of Power and coming on the clouds of
heaven." (Matthew 26:63–64)

By this time the entire Sanhedrin has been gathered in
the dark hours before daybreak. For quite some time the
members of this religious court of justice had wanted to kill
Jesus of Nazareth. This was their chance to convict Him.
But no crime could be found. False witnesses testified, but
none could agree, for Jesus is the perfect, innocent Second
Adam. He remained silent to the fraudulent charges. Finally,
Caiaphas, in desperation, demanded Jesus to answer
under oath. Was He the Messiah promised by God? Jesus
in majestic eloquence speaks His "yes," convicting the high
priest with his own words. Christ confesses His deity, using
strong prophetic words from the Old Testament.

The rejection by the Jewish hierarchy does not change
who this Christ before them is. Their rejection of Him
will not be the end, but the beginning of a new era. He
is the Judge that will come in heavenly clouds to convict
unbelievers of their sin. They will be declared guilty,
sentenced to eternal death. He is also the Shepherd that
gathers in His arms all who believe in the forgiveness of
sins. At the same time He is the Lamb of God who will in a
few short hours lay down His life to redeem His sheep and
thereby open heaven. In the blood of Christ we are declared
innocent and holy; we are justified and given the gift of
eternal life.

Stricken, smitten, and afflicted,
    See Him dying on the tree!
'Tis the Christ, by man rejected;
    Yes, my soul, 'tis He, 'tis He!
'Tis the long expected Prophet,
    David's Son, yet David's Lord;
Proofs I see sufficient of it:
    'Tis the true and faithful Word.

Tell me, ye who hear Him groaning,
    Was there ever grief like His?
Friends through fear His cause disowning,
    Foes insulting His distress;
Many hands were raised to wound Him,
    None would intervene to save;
But the deepest stroke that pierced Him
    Was the stroke that justice gave.

Ye who think of sin but lightly
    Nor suppose the evil great
Here may view its nature rightly,
    Here its guilt may estimate.
Mark the sacrifice appointed,
    See who bears the awful load;
'Tis the Word, the Lord's anointed,
    Son of Man and Son of God.

Here we have a firm foundation,
    Here the refuge of the lost:
Christ, the Rock of our salvation,
    Is the name of which we boast;
Lamb of God, for sinners wounded,
    Sacrifice to cancel guilt!
None shall ever be confounded
    Who on Him their hope have built.
            (*LSB* 451:1–4)

Mocking of Christ

The Mocking of Christ

Luke 22:63–65

After Jesus was found guilty of blasphemy and condemned to death by Caiaphas, He is subjected to torture and indignity by the hands of the soldiers. Various tormentors surround the blindfolded Christ. They taunt Him, demanding that He prove His godly Sonship. He is cruelly struck on the head and face, verbally insulted in mock homage, and spit upon. Dürer adds a painful auditory torture, depicting a musician that blasts a horn in the ear of Christ.

We see, front and center, our Savior for His night of mockery. He grips His knees but otherwise sits passively in the midst of His terrorists, enduring both emotional and physical pain. A scantily clad figure in the lower left corner, coolly eating his dinner, simply watches Christ's ordeal. This onlooker, below whom rests Dürer's monogram, places you at the feet of Jesus. Through all of this, Jesus, the incarnate Son of God, remains silent and in control as He willingly takes our punishment, humiliation, and sin into His own body.

> Now the men who were holding Jesus in custody were mocking Him as they beat Him. They also blindfolded Him and kept asking Him, "Prophesy! Who is it that struck you?" And they said many other things against Him, blaspheming Him. (Luke 22:63–65)

The trial with the Sanhedrin was over. The verdict: blasphemy! The sentence: death! However, the religious court at that time had no jurisdiction over political matters of execution. They would need to wait until morning to take the prisoner to the Roman authority. Until then, time is spent in wicked, perverted games. The soldiers now have free rein to make cruel sport of Him in the courtyard of the high priest. They are Satan's agents as they mock and abuse the Messiah promised by God throughout the Old Testament.

Several times during His ministry, Jesus had prophesied His entire Passion. Now blindfolded, Jesus is mockingly asked to prophesy the names of His tormentors. Our omnipotent Lord could have spoken not only their names, but even the number of hairs on their heads. Instead He remains silent. He endures the physical and emotional shame for us. We live in a sinful world. Sadly, each of us has suffered cruel mistreatment at the hands and mouths of others. And equally, each of us has sinned against our neighbors in cruel thoughts, words, and deeds. Our sin clings to every aspect of our lives. But there is forgiveness! Our Savior has taken all sins to the cross—those we have done, and those sins done against us. What great news! Christ has removed our sin and its shame. "The blood of Jesus His Son cleanses us from all sin" (1 John 1:7).

Christ, the life of all the living,
  Christ, the death of death, our foe,
Who, Thyself for me once giving
  To the darkest depths of woe:
Through Thy suff'rings, death, and merit
I eternal life inherit.
    Thousand, thousand thanks shall be,
    Dearest Jesus, unto Thee.

Thou, ah! Thou, hast taken on Thee
  Bonds and stripes, a cruel rod;
Pain and scorn were heaped upon Thee,
  Oh Thou sinless Son of God!
Thus didst Thou my soul deliver
From the bonds of sin forever.
    Thousand, thousand thanks shall be,
    Dearest Jesus, unto Thee.
                    (*LSB* 420:1–2)

Christ before Pilate

CHRIST BEFORE PILATE

John 18:28–38

Though it is early morning, the darkness of evil continues. The third trial in the Passion of Christ is held outside the palace of Pontius Pilate, the Roman procurator of Judea. Ordinary Renaissance houses of the sixteenth century peek through the windows of the Praetorium, the governor's headquarters, allowing contemporary man a view of the proceedings. Although the Jewish leaders have convicted Jesus of blasphemy and sentenced Him to death, they have no authority to carry out the death penalty. They appeal to the civil ruler to legalize their wicked plan.

Placed in the corner by Dürer, the high priest dominates the woodcut by his large size. He counts on his fingers the various charges against Jesus, chief of which are treason and sedition by His claim as king. "We found this man misleading our nation and forbidding us to give tribute to Caesar, and saying that He Himself is Christ, a king" (Luke 23:2). Satan, a devilish looking spectator, completes the corner vignette. He relaxes at the Jewish ruler's feet, profile lit in a smile. The rat-like features of the little dog between him and Jesus are symbolic of evil. Pilate, after examining Jesus and finding the charges invalid, lifts his hand in peace to calm the multitude, saying "I find no guilt in this man" (Luke 23:4). Instead, upon hearing his words, the crowd becomes fiercer.

Jesus, barefoot, surrounded by armed guards, and with rope bound around His neck, is placed at the edge of the scene. Although portrayed considerably larger than His captors, Christ remains silent and peaceful, resolute in His journey to the cross. He stands as an innocent spectator to the court proceedings that will lead to His death.

> Then Pilate said to Him, "So You are a King?" Jesus answered, "You say that I am a king. For this purpose I was born and for this purpose I have come into the world—to bear witness to the truth. Everyone who is of the truth listens to My voice." Pilate said to Him, "What is truth?" After he had said this, he went back outside to the Jews and told them, "I find no guilt in Him." (John 18:37–38)

The members of the Sanhedrin were determined to rid themselves of this Jesus of Nazareth. In their hardened hearts they believed He had convicted Himself of blasphemy in His claim as the Son of God. He deserved death. They would stop at nothing less. In order that the execution be legal, it needed to be carried out under Roman authority. Early on Friday morning of Christ's Passion, He is taken as a bound criminal to the palace of Pontius Pilate. The Jewish leaders ask for the death penalty. But their religious charge, masked as political insurrection, does not ring true. Pilate takes Jesus inside for a private interview and is confronted by Christ the King, "the way, and the truth, and the life" (John 14:6).

Jesus' kingdom is not an earthly one. He rules men's hearts with the truth of God's saving love. He is the King who was born to die on a cross, to destroy the evil that began in the Garden of Eden. Pilate asks: "What is truth?" And the truth is we are all sinners who have rejected God. We deserve nothing but punishment and death. The truth is the innocent Son of God who came to take our punishment and death into His own body. He came to exchange our sin and guilt for His innocence. Pilate's words are true: "I find no guilt in Him." And yet Christ bears the guilt of all!

> Thou hast borne the smiting only
> > That my wounds might all be whole;
> Thou hast suffered, sad and lonely,
> > Rest to give my weary soul;
> Yea, the curse of God enduring,
> Blessing unto me securing.
> > Thousand, thousand thanks shall be,
> > Dearest Jesus, unto Thee.
>
> Heartless scoffers did surround Thee,
> > Treating Thee with shameful scorn
> And with piercing thorns they crowned Thee.
> > All disgrace Thou, Lord, hast borne,
> That as Thine Thou mightest own me
> And with heav'nly glory crown me.
> > Thousand, thousand thanks shall be,
> > Dearest Jesus, unto Thee.
> > > (*LSB* 420:3–4)

Christ before Herod

CHRIST BEFORE HEROD

Luke 23:6–12

Pilate's dilemma is a difficult one. To satisfy the angry rulers of the Jews, he must condemn the innocent Jesus. He finds a temporary solution by shifting the responsibility to Herod Antipas. Let the tetrarch of Galilee decide the fate of this Galilean man! The prison bars under the throne in this woodcut remind the viewer of the cruel imprisonment and beheading of another prophet, John the Baptist, who publicly denounced Herod's sin of adultery.

In this print, Dürer centers on three individuals, each portraying a different emotion. The priest is livid, his accusing gestures adamant as he attempts to convince Herod that Christ is guilty and must die for His crimes. But Herod's face is puzzled and bewildered as he begs and cajoles for sensational, supernatural entertainment. Although he is seated on a throne with scepter in hand, this earthly king is powerless before the King of creation. Even the little dog at the ruler's feet lies in submission. Jesus, bound with rope around neck and hands, remains in dignified silence. "He was oppressed, and He was afflicted, yet He opened not His mouth; like a lamb that is led to the slaughter, and like a sheep before its shearers is silent, so He opened not His mouth" (Isaiah 53:7). The sinless Son of Man, his expression one of perfect control, willingly journeys to the cross to pay for the sins of guilty mankind.

> When Herod saw Jesus, he was very glad, for he
> had long desired to see Him, because he had
> heard about Him, and he was hoping to see some
> sign done by Him. So he questioned Him at some
> length, but He made no answer. (Luke 23:8–9)

Even though Pilate knows Jesus is innocent, he does not have the courage to set Him free. Herod was in Jerusalem for the Passover, and so instead of making the determination himself, Pilate transfers the troublesome case to Herod, who has jurisdiction over the region and people of Galilee. Herod is thrilled! He has heard that Jesus of Nazareth performed miracles—that he healed the sick, fed thousands of people with a few loaves of bread, and, most astonishingly, raised the dead. Herod wants entertainment. He wants magic tricks and a show from this Galilean.

This is the same temptation Satan offered to Jesus at the beginning of His ministry, when "he took Him to Jerusalem and set Him on the pinnacle of the temple and said to Him, 'If You are the Son of God, throw Yourself down from here, for it is written, 'He will command His angels concerning You, to guard You' " (Luke 4:9–10). Jesus, the omnipotent Son of God, could have complied with Herod's begging and perform a miracle. He could have saved His life. He could have gone free. But He did not! For in doing so He would have become an earthly king and forfeited the cross. He remained silent and still for you and me. His heart was set on His life as our ransom. Little did Herod know that in a few short hours, the greatest miracle in all of history would take place. God would die on a cross to pay for the sins of all mankind—Herod's sin, your sin, and my sin.

Thou hast suffered men to bruise Thee,
    That from pain I might be free;
Falsely did Thy foes accuse Thee:
    Thence I gain security;
Comfortless Thy soul did languish
Me to comfort in my anguish.
        Thousand, thousand thanks shall be,
        Dearest Jesus, unto Thee.

Thou hast suffered great affliction
    And hast borne it patiently,
Even death by crucifixion,
    Fully to atone for me;
Thou didst choose to be tormented
That my doom should be prevented.
        Thousand, thousand thanks shall be,
        Dearest Jesus, unto Thee.

Then, for all that wrought my pardon,
    For Thy sorrows deep and sore,
For Thine anguish in the Garden,
    I will thank Thee evermore,
Thank Thee for Thy groaning, sighing,
For Thy bleeding and Thy dying,
        For that last triumphant cry,
        And shall praise Thee, Lord, on high.
                (LSB 420:5–7)

Flagellation

The Flagellation

John 19:1

Here in this woodcut we see Jesus once again under Pilate's jurisdiction. The Roman ruler tries one more time to divert the insistent Jews from their evil plan, meant to destroy an innocent man. He appeals to their sense of pity. Flogging, the standard prologue to crucifixion, shreds the flesh from Jesus' back and begins the death process. Jesus is tied to a pillar of the Praetorium and stripped to a loincloth. He is seen for the last time before His death with the strong body of a carpenter.

Though He must endure public humiliation and the excruciating pain of scourging, Christ's face is resolute in submission. Pilate, eyes averted and arms crossed, is depicted as a bystander who wants to have no part in this wicked crime. Yet he is the authority who ordered this punishment. The Renaissance house, seen above the wall, places contemporary man as a witness and participant in this scandalous event. Two guards, their actions brutally animated, wield instruments of torture, but the third has dropped his tool of death, an incriminating finger pointed downward to Dürer's initials, carved in stone at the feet of Christ. We are all guilty of His suffering and death.

> [Pilate] went back outside to the Jews and told
> them, "I find no guilt in Him. But you have a
> custom that I should release one man for you at
> the Passover. So do you want me to release to you
> the King of the Jews?" They cried out again, "Not
> this man, but Barabbas!" Now Barabbas was a
> robber. Then Pilate took Jesus and flogged Him.
> (John 18:38b–19:1)

Herod, not wanting to involve himself with the Jewish
religious leaders by condemning Jesus, has sent Jesus back
to Pilate. Let the Roman official bear the responsibility of
this troublesome case! But Pilate, too, is a coward. He lacks
the courage to go against the Jews. He lacks the courage to
defend the man he knew to be innocent. Instead he becomes
an unjust judge. He releases Barabbas, a known murderer,
hoping to appease the crowd. Yet the vindictive mob is
not satisfied. Pilate takes another step and begins the
crucifixion process by ordering Christ to be flogged. Surely
this punishment will satisfy the people.

Scourging was reserved for slaves and dangerous
criminals; often they died during this severe punishment;
it was more than whipping. Metal shards tied to leather
cords ripped the victim's flesh open to the bone in agonizing
torture. When used as a precursor to crucifixion, scourging
intensified the experience of being crucified. Roman
executioners were experts at their task, ensuring that the
condemned did not die prematurely during the ordeal. The
flogging of Christ is prophesied in Psalm 129:3: "The plowers
plowed upon My back; they made long their furrows."

Why does Christ allow this? Why does the sinless Son
of God allow His body to be painfully torn to shreds? He

willingly bears the curse of death that began in the Garden of Eden. This is the curse that we all bear in our bodies, from the moment of conception. Have you suffered pain? Does your body fail you? Are you sick? Are you weak? Do you hurt? Our Savior knows our sufferings. He knows how it feels because He has felt pain. He has felt incredible, debilitating weakness. Jesus, in His truly human body, has born the greatest suffering that mankind will ever endure. Why? Because our Lord loves us! Christ suffered to save us from an eternity of suffering in hell. He took our punishment that we might have eternal peace in body and soul. "But He was pierced for our transgressions; He was crushed for our iniquities; upon Him was the chastisement that brought us peace, and with His wounds we are healed" (Isaiah 53:5).

> O dearest Jesus, what law hast Thou broken
> That such sharp sentence should on Thee be spoken?
> Of what great crime hast Thou to make confession,
> What dark transgression?
>
> They crown Thy head with thorns, they smite, they scourge Thee;
> With cruel mockings to the cross they urge Thee;
> They give Thee gall to drink, they still decry Thee;
> They crucify Thee.
>
> Whence come these sorrows, whence this mortal anguish?
> It is my sins for which Thou, Lord, must languish;
> Yea, all the wrath, the woe, Thou dost inherit,
> This I do merit.
>
> The sinless Son of God must die in sadness;
> The sinful child of man may live in gladness;
> Man forfeited his life and is acquitted;
> God is committed.
>
> (*LSB* 439:1–3, 5)

Christ Crowned with Thorns

CHRIST CROWNED WITH THORNS

Matthew 27:27–31

After scourging, the degradation of Christ continues. In the courtyard of the Praetorium, the Roman soldiers make cruel sport of His kingship. They dress Jesus as royalty, with both robe and crown, to engage in the physical and emotional torture of mock homage. Jesus, face haggard and body wounded, sits in somber dignity on a pseudo-throne. His hand willingly accepts the reed scepter as His eyes sadly and lovingly gaze at the kneeler who doffs his hat in fake worship. The mocker's face is ugly. He spits at Christ, taunting, "Hail, King of the Jews!" (Matthew 27:29b). The plaited wreath of thorns is jabbed into the head of Christ while another soldier inflicts harsh blows with a stick. Pilate stands in back, conversing with a spectator. Although his face is turned away, the stick in his hand clearly implicates him as a participant in the evil proceedings.

Dürer's portrayal of this account moves the heart of the viewer to sorrow, disgust, and lamentation in recognition that we are all participants in Adam's rejection of God. "He was despised and rejected by men; a man of sorrows and acquainted with grief; and as one from whom men hide their faces; He was despised, and we esteemed Him not" (Isaiah 53:3).

And they stripped Him and put a scarlet robe on
Him, and twisting together a crown of thorns,
they put it on His head and put a reed in His right
hand. And kneeling before Him, they mocked
Him, saying, "Hail, King of the Jews!" And they spit
on Him and took the reed and struck Him on the
head. (Matthew 27:28–30)

The Passion of our Lord intensifies with physical and
emotional cruelty. The Jews had mocked Jesus earlier.
Now, under Pilate's authority, the Roman soldiers delight
in mocking a man claiming to be king of a people they
despise. Yet it is here we see the Suffering Servant come
into His kingship. All the royal elements are present—robe,
crown, scepter, and homage, though perverted. Rather than
reigning in pomp and power, this King sits in weakness and
submission. His robe is not lined with satin, but is saturated
with the blood needed to pay for our sins. His crown is not
studded with jewels, but is adorned with thorns, resting
on a head meant to bear our punishment. His scepter is
not golden and silver, but is a green reed designed to break
our bondage. His homage is not stately and regal, but
humiliating and degrading; yet the mocker's spit cannot
stop Him from honoring us as forgiven sons and daughters.

Here we see the ugly cost of sin. Here we see our
beautiful Savior's love for us. He bears mankind's sin in
order to release us from the torments of our physical and
emotional pain. Here we see the Father's love for us as He
offers His Son to death for our life. "He Himself bore our
sins in His body on the tree, that we might die to sin and
live to righteousness. By His wounds you have been healed"
(1 Peter 2:24).

O sacred Head, now wounded,
With grief and shame weighed down,
Now scornfully surrounded
With thorns, Thine only crown.
O sacred Head, what glory,
What bliss, till now was Thine!
Yet, though despised and gory,
I joy to call Thee mine.

How pale Thou art with anguish,
With sore abuse and scorn!
How doth Thy face now languish
That once was bright as morn!
Grim death, with cruel rigor,
Hath robbed Thee of Thy life;
Thus Thou hast lost Thy vigor,
Thy strength, in this sad strife.

What Thou, my Lord, hast suffered
Was all for sinners' gain;
Mine, mine was the transgression,
But Thine the deadly pain.
Lo, here I fall, my Savior!
'Tis I deserve Thy place;
Look on me with Thy favor,
And grant to me Thy grace.

Be Thou my consolation,
My shield, when I must die;
Remind me of Thy passion
When my last hour draws nigh.
Mine eyes shall then behold Thee,
Upon Thy cross shall dwell,
My heart by faith enfold Thee.
Who dieth thus dies well.

(*LSB* 450:1–3, 7)

Ecce Homo

ECCE HOMO

John 19:4–16

Pilate makes his third attempt to free Jesus. A large Romanesque window is used as a small stage for showcasing the wounded Christ. Pilate hopes to influence the crowd by appealing to their sense of compassion and justice. "Ecce Homo—Behold the Man!" But the mob will not be swayed.

In the foreground, Jewish leaders have their hands upraised. Opposite, a man of the Renaissance period chimes in with their cry. Even the Roman soldier guarding Christ is shouting, "Crucify Him, crucify Him!" Priests stand to the side with a cross and ladder, ready for the execution. As the insistent and angry mob continues demanding death, Pilate makes his final plea. Holding a scepter, symbolic of his authority, he points to Jesus. The other hand, pointing to himself, declares again the verdict of innocence. But the evil cannot be stopped. Center front, a man holding a halberd, a fifteenth-century weapon of war, crouches in fear and confusion as the battle over life and death rages. This onlooker, between Christ and the Dürer monogram, places you as witness to the greatest injustice in all of history. In the midst of this chaos, the Son of God remains in calm resignation, reed scepter in hand. The three-pronged halo denotes His divinity as the Son of God. At the same time, wearing a crown of thorns, His body stripped of clothing, and a rope binding His neck and hands, He shows His humanity as the Son of Man. "Behold, the Lamb of God, who takes away the sin of the world!" (John 1:29).

[Pilate] entered his headquarters again and said to

Jesus, "Where are You from?" But Jesus gave him no answer. So Pilate said to Him, "You will not speak to me? Do You not know that I have authority to release You and authority to crucify You?" Jesus answered him, "You would have no authority over Me at all unless it had been given you from above. Therefore he who delivered Me over to you has the greater sin." (John 19:9–11)

In the last trial of Christ's Passion we see the universal rejection of the Savior of the world. Although Pilate knows Jesus is innocent, his fear and cowardice give way to the Jews' hatred. Without realizing it, Pilate speaks the profound truth of God's plan of salvation: "Behold the man . . . behold your King!" (John 19:5, 14). This pitiful, weak, bloodied, thorn-crowned man standing before them is none other than God Himself. He takes into His innocent flesh the sins of the world. Who is guilty of this injustice to the Son of God? Who is responsible for killing Christ? Pilate? Caiaphas? The Sanhedrin? Judas? Adam and Eve? You and me? We are all guilty! We have all betrayed our God. We all seek our own evil, self-centered ways. We all sin against our God and our neighbor. We cannot help ourselves. We are caught in sin and, try as we might, there is no way out.

But here we have comfort in the words of Jesus: "You would have no authority over Me at all unless it had been given you from above" (John 19:11a). The mob, the chaos, the hatred, the blood—everything looks out of control and destined for evil. And yet our Savior is in perfect control. He is the obedient Son carrying out His Father's plan to rescue sinners from eternal death—Gentiles and Jews, you and me. "All we like sheep have gone astray; we have turned—

everyone—to his own way; and the LORD has laid on Him the iniquity of us all" (Isaiah 53:6).

O perfect life of love!
    All, all, is finished now,
All that he left His throne above
    To do for us below.

No work is left undone
    Of all the Father willed;
His toil, His sorrows, one by one,
    The Scriptures have fulfilled.

No pain that we can share
    But He has felt its smart;
All forms of human grief and care
    Have pierced that tender heart.

And on His thorn-crowned head
    And on His sinless soul
Our sins in all their guilt were laid
    That He might make us whole.

In perfect love He dies;
    For me He dies, for me.
O all-atoning Sacrifice,
    I cling by faith to Thee.

In ev'ry time of need,
    Before the judgment throne,
Thy work, O Lamb of God, I'll plead,
    Thy merits, not mine own.
            (*LSB* 452:1–6)

Pilate Washing His Hands

Pilate Washing His Hands

Matthew 27:15–26

The trial is over. The criminal is condemned. Christ and Pontius Pilate are separated. The scene is the "judgment seat at a place called The Stone Pavement, and in Aramaic Gabbatha" (John 19:13). Two actions of the Passion narrative are taking place simultaneously in the Dürer print. In one half, the Roman procurator washes his hands in a show of symbolic innocence, attended and witnessed by his servants. Pilate's eyes are downcast as he ponders the incredible horror of his verdict. By succumbing to his fear of losing his government position and career, he has betrayed his own inner sense of justice. Dire consequence will follow. The water brings no soothing cleansing. The words of his wife's warning echo in his troubled conscience: "Have nothing to do with that righteous man, for I have suffered much because of Him today in a dream" (Matthew 27:19).

On the other side of the scene, armed guards escort Jesus, a rope about His neck, from the courtyard. He continues His journey to the cross without protest. In His death our Savior becomes the living water, a fountain of cleansing for all mankind's sins.

So when Pilate saw that he was gaining nothing,
but rather that a riot was beginning, he took
water and washed his hands before the crowd,
saying, "I am innocent of this man's blood; see to
it yourselves." And all the people answered, "His
blood be on us and on our children!" (Matthew
27:24–25)

Pilate knew in his heart that Jesus was not guilty of any
crime. He proclaimed the innocence of Christ to the crowd
time and again during the trials. Even his wife tried to
intervene on behalf of that pure and noble man. But Pilate's
fear of the people sells out his sense of justice. He knowingly
condemns the faultless Jesus of Nazareth to death. The
guilt is enormous. He has to do something to rid himself
of the responsibility of the crime he committed, so he tries
to cleanse himself from his sin. In washing his hands he
attempts to dump his guilt on the people.

Does this sound familiar? It is the same sin of Adam in
the Garden of Eden. Rather than confessing his sin to God,
Adam attempts to dump his guilt on Eve, and, ultimately,
on God. We are all like Adam. We are all like Pilate. None of
us wants to admit our sin. None of us wants to feel the guilt.
It feels horrible, heavy, and loathsome. We can't bear it! So
our God bears the weight of sin for us. In Christ, the sinless
Son of God, all our guilt is nailed to the cross, crucified and
buried in the grave. In Baptism we rise with Christ to new
life, our hearts cleansed by His blood, for "God shows His
love for us in that while we were still sinners, Christ died for
us. Since therefore, we have now been justified by His blood,
much more shall we be saved by Him from the wrath of
God" (Romans 5:8–9).

Come to Calv'ry's holy mountain,
　　Sinners, ruined by the fall;
Here a pure and healing fountain
　　Flows for you, for me, for all,
In a full, perpetual tide,
Opened when our Savior died.

Come in poverty and meanness,
　　Come defiled, without, within;
From infection and uncleanness,
　　From the leprosy of sin,
Wash your robes and make them white;
Ye shall walk with God in light.

Come in sorrow and contrition,
　　Wounded, impotent, and blind;
Here the guilty, free remission,
　　Here the troubled, peace, may find.
Health this fountain will restore;
They that drink shall thirst no more.

They that drink shall live forever;
　　'Tis a soul-renewing flood.
God is faithful; God will never
　　Break His covenant of blood,
Signed when our Redeemer died,
Sealed when He was glorified.
　　　　　　　　　(*LSB* 435:1–4)

Bearing of the Cross

BEARING OF THE CROSS

Luke 23:26–31

A chaotic mob follows the convicted Christ outside the walls of Jerusalem as the macabre processional moves toward Calvary. Jesus is weak from a night of trials, hungry and weary from the public humiliation, degradation, and mocking, flogged and severely beaten. Still bearing the crown of thorns, He collapses under the heavy weight of bearing the cross. A soldier goads Him on, jabbing His neck with a spear, but Jesus stops for one last teaching on repentance. The Savior's upturned face is filled with pity and grave concern, not for Himself, but for the weeping women. Despite His own impending execution, He mourns for those who lament His death. Even though His own destruction looms near, He warns them of the destruction of Jerusalem.

Beside the cross a soldier carries the prisoner's neck rope and the basket of tools used in a crucifixion. Simon of Cyrene supports the lower end of the cross while John and Mary follow closely behind, their saddened faces downcast. Smug priests, riding on horseback, preside over the evil moment. A satanic looking man transports the ladder, and behind him the city gate is closed. There is no turning back. The Son willingly journeys the last road to complete the Father's plan of salvation. In the corner, Dürer's trademark insignia is attached to the cross of Christ.

> And as they led Him away, they seized one Simon
> of Cyrene, who was coming in from the country,
> and laid on him the cross, to carry it behind Jesus.
> (Luke 23:26)

The contrast between Christ's entry into Jerusalem and His exit from the city is astonishing. The royal road draped in garments and festooned with palm branches is now stained with blood. Rejoicing has given way to weeping. The song "Hosanna to the Son of David" has become the death cry, "Crucify Him!" The King riding a colt is now a condemned criminal, stumbling under the heavy weight of a cross. Jesus is suffering physically from a night of torture and trials. He is suffering emotionally with the weight of mankind's sin and guilt.

Seeing Him collapse, Roman soldiers compel a bystander to carry His cross. Simon of Cyrene becomes a participant in the procession to Calvary. He is a picture of what all followers of Christ must do. "If anyone would come after Me, let him deny himself and take up his cross daily and follow Me" (Luke 9:23). What does it mean to deny ourselves? What does it mean to take up the cross? We look to our crucified Lord. To follow Him is to suffer with Him. This suffering is not to pay for our sins. Christ has already done that for us. We are told by Christ that we, too, will bear a cross, yet our suffering is not to suffer as He did—even though it may bring our death. Our suffering comes as we live out our lives as Christians. Our suffering is to bear rejection on account of Christ, as Christ has borne rejection for us. But there is hope! There is comfort. Just as God used the suffering of Christ for good, He promises to bring good from our suffering. In the shadow of the cross we cling to

Christ, where the world's greatest suffering has already taken place. It is done. No matter what cross we must bear, we are safe in Christ.

A Lamb goes uncomplaining forth,
    The guilt of sinners bearing
And, laden with the sins of earth,
    None else the burden sharing;
Goes patient on, grows weak and faint,
To slaughter led without complaint,
    That spotless life to offer,
He bears the stripes, the wounds, the lies,
The mockery, and yet replies,
    "All this I gladly suffer."

This Lamb is Christ, the soul's great friend,
    The Lamb of God, our Savior,
Whom God the Father chose to send
    To gain for us His favor.
"Go forth, My Son," the Father said,
"And free My children from their dread
    Of guilt and condemnation.
The wrath and stripes are hard to bear,
But by Your passion they will share
    The fruit of Your salvation."
            (*LSB* 438:1–2)

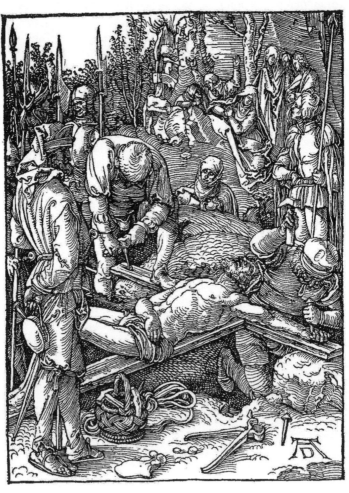

Christ Nailed to the Cross

CHRIST NAILED TO THE CROSS

John 19:16–18

None of the Gospels provide any details for the process of crucifixion. Most likely, the evangelists didn't need to, as early Christians would have been familiar with the gruesome protocol. They had perhaps even been eyewitnesses to the common Roman practice of execution. Dürer, however, visualizes Psalm 22:16 with heart wrenching poignancy: "They have pierced My hands and feet."

The viewer sees every detail of the crucifixion as soldiers wield drill, hammer, and spikes to fasten our Lord to the cross. The tools of the carpenter now become tools of torture. Open pincers lay on the ground, awaiting death and the final removal of the nails. Arm resting peacefully across His body, Jesus endures excruciating pain as He calmly waits for the last nail to be driven home. The tool basket is reminiscent of the basket pictured by Dürer in the Nativity woodcut. Once cradling the infant Christ Child, the Incarnate God who came to earth to die so that mankind might live, the basket now holds the very instruments used by those who are delivering Him to death.

In the background, the faithful women keep watch. Though one is seen in prayer, the others huddle in shock and horror near the disciple John. Yet the composure of our Savior is amazing. He is not a victim struggling for freedom, but is rather obedient in his surrender, willingly giving up His life to death.

> And when they came to the place that is called The
> Skull, there they crucified Him, and the criminals,
> one on His right and one on His left. And Jesus
> said, "Father, forgive them, for they know not what
> they do." And they cast lots to divide His garments.
> (Luke 23:33–34)

The journey is over. Christ has reached His destination. His innocent life ends in a humiliating, agonizing death, reserved for slaves guilty of the worst crimes. Though we are the guilty slaves, and we are those guilty of the worst crimes, having rebelled against God and deserving of the punishment, Jesus takes our place. He takes our punishment for sin into His body. There is no struggle, only compliance as Jesus, true God and true Man, willingly lets Himself be crucified for you and me. As Passover lambs were being ritually sacrificed in the temple courtyard, the Lamb of God, the ultimate Passover Lamb, is sacrificed outside of the city on Calvary's cross to pay for the sins of the world. Jesus, the sinless Son of God, is nailed to a cross to be hung between two sinners, for "He poured out His soul to death and was numbered with the transgressors" (Isaiah 53:12).

Jesus came to live with sinners. He teaches them. He eats with them. He heals them. Jesus came to die for sinners and with sinners. His first words from the cross are for sinners. He prays for sinners. He asks His Father to forgive those who are killing Him—the Roman soldiers, the Jewish leaders, His disciples, Adam and Eve, and you and me. Such amazing love! There is no condemnation. Only forgiveness. The death of Christ not only forgives our sin, but dramatically teaches us what forgiveness is—to love and pray for those who hurt us. Our Savior not only pays the price for our sins, but by His death teaches us how to love and to live.

> Lamb of God, pure and holy,
> > Who on the cross didst suffer,
> Ever patient and lowly,
> > Thyself to scorn didst offer.
> All sins Thou borest for us,
> Else had despair reigned o'er us:
> > Have mercy on us, O Jesus! O Jesus!
>
> Lamb of God, pure and holy,
> > Who on the cross didst suffer,
> Ever patient and lowly,
> > Thyself to scorn didst offer.
> All sins Thou borest for us,
> Else had despair reigned o'er us:
> > Thy peace be with us, O Jesus! O Jesus!
> > > (*LSB* 434: 1, 3)

Crucifixion

THE CRUCIFIXION

Matthew 27:33–56

The cross of Christ, which is the heart and center of the Christian Church, dominates the eerie afternoon darkness of this woodcut. Beneath the inscription "Jesus of Nazareth, the King of the Jews," the nimbus and crown of thorns proclaim the Savior's divine and human natures (John 19:19). The skull at the bottom symbolizes not only the location of the crucifixion, Golgotha, which means, according to Matthew 27:33, "Place of a Skull," but is an icon for Adam. It is nestled in a tree root growing from the foot of the cross. The obedient Second Adam gives His life in payment for the disobedience of the first Adam and his descendants that first began with the tree in the garden. The crucified body of Christ is both the fulfillment of the curse, "for the wages of sin is death," and the fulfillment of the promise, "but the free gift of God is eternal life in Christ Jesus our Lord" (Romans 6:23).

Although it is common in Renaissance art to see Mary Magdalene kneeling at the cross, kissing Jesus' feet, this is not recorded in Scripture. Rather, it is based on the tradition that she was the sinful woman who anointed Jesus' feet in Luke 7:36–50. The Bible only states that she was present at the crucifixion, along with other women.

In this image, the cross divides two groups of people, signifying the two main doctrines of Scripture. For the scoffers and mockers on Christ's left, the cross brings the Law and, through it, death. For the faithful followers on the opposite side, the cross brings the Gospel and eternal life. This is emphasized by the right hand placement of Jesus' pierced side, flowing with the blood of the Lord's Supper and the waters of Baptism. "But one of the soldiers pierced His side with a spear, and at once there came out blood and water" (John 19:34). Through the wounds of Christ, the healing gifts of forgiveness, life, and salvation are freely given to all believers.

> Now from the sixth hour there was darkness over all the land until the ninth hour. And about the ninth hour Jesus cried out with a loud voice, saying "*Eli, Eli, lema sabachthani?*" that is, "My God, My God, why have You forsaken Me?" (Matthew 27:45–46)

God entered time for this very moment! The Son of God entered into our human history to take our place on a shameful cross. It is a scandalous, earthshaking event. Seeing the King of creation hanging naked on a tree, the sun refuses to shine. All of creation is in chaotic horror. The black of night descends. The prince of darkness reigns. The Savior bears the curse of our sin. He pays the price of our abandoning God that began in the Garden of Eden and continues in our lives today. He bears the wrath of God that we deserve. And He defeats Satan for us.

God is holy; He hates sin. God is just; thus sin must be paid for. But God is also love! Rather than killing the sinner, He places our sin and guilt on His Son. The almighty God turns His back on His sinless, obedient Son and offers Him as the perfect sacrifice meant to redeem all of mankind. On the cross Jesus suffers the punishment of hell for us. He is forsaken by His Father so we will never be forsaken. No matter what darkness we face in our lives, we have the promise that God is with us. "For He has said, 'I will never leave you nor forsake you.' So we can confidently say,

'The Lord is my helper; I will not fear; what can man do to me?' " (Hebrews 13:5–6). Faith clings to our Savior. In the crucifixion of Christ, God no longer holds our sins against us. Our sin is exchanged for His holiness. In the cross we are justified and declared innocent before God.

> Cross of Jesus, cross of sorrow,
>> Where the blood of Christ was shed,
> Perfect man on thee did suffer,
>> Perfect God on thee has bled!
>
> Here the King of all the ages,
>> Throned in light ere worlds could be,
> Robed in mortal flesh is dying,
>> Crucified by sin for me.
>
> O mysterious condescending!
>> O abandonment sublime!
> Very God Himself is bearing
>> All the sufferings of time!
>
> Cross of Jesus, cross of sorrow,
>> Where the blood of Christ was shed,
> Perfect man on thee did suffer,
>> Perfect God on thee has bled!
>>> (*LSB* 428:1–4)

Descent from the Cross

DESCENT FROM THE CROSS

John 19:38–40

The soldiers are gone. The crowd has dispersed. The priests and scribes have retreated to the temple, confident that the troublemaker is gone. "It is better for you that one man should die for the people, not that the whole nation should perish" (John 11:50). A tree in the background of the woodcut brings to remembrance the tree in the Garden of Eden, and Adam's sin that brought death into the world. Only the followers of Jesus remain. They pay homage to their dead Lord by taking care of His body.

The scene is tender. The crown of thorns has been removed and hangs from the cross. Joseph of Arimathea, a secret disciple, had boldly asked Pilate's permission to bury Jesus. Now he stands ready with a linen shroud. Nicodemus, dressed as a man of the Renaissance, ascends the ladder. He embraces the corpse of Christ, draping the weight of His upper body over his shoulders. Another faithful follower steadies the beloved body with a long strip of cloth. Below, a disciple uses pincers to remove the spikes that held the Savior's feet fast to the cross. The wounds from the nails are enormous. The hammer still lies close by, having been used just six hours earlier. The women appear muted in the background, overcome with the evil proceedings of the day. Jesus Christ is dead.

He said, "It is finished," and He bowed His head and gave up His spirit. (John 19:30)

It's done! It's over! The sins of all mankind from Adam and Eve until the end of time are paid for by the death of the incarnate Son of God. Jesus has taken all the evils and woes of the entire world into His body and paid for them with His holy, precious blood. He willingly gave His life for us. He died because He wanted to die. He died because this was the Father's plan to destroy sin without destroying the sinner. With a loud cry, Jesus announced that God's plan of salvation is accomplished. Sin is defeated! There is nothing we can do or have to do to pay the price of our sin. God has done it all for us through the death of His Son. What comfort this is for the heart and conscience tortured with guilt.

But what if I don't feel forgiven? Look to the cross. Listen to Christ's words: "It is finished." Forgiveness does not depend on our feelings. We believe we are forgiven because our Savior tells us it is so. Satan wants to rob us of God's gifts. Just as he did with Adam and Eve in the Garden of Eden, he still comes to each of us with his lies. He wants us to doubt God's words of forgiveness. He wants us to feel that the death of Jesus is not enough. He wants us to believe that God still counts our sins against us. Praise God, salvation depends not on our feelings or works, but on the work of Christ for us! It is finished!

Thy works, not mine, O Christ,
Speak gladness to this heart;
They tell me all is done,
They bid my fear depart.

*(Refrain)*To whom save Thee,
Who canst alone
For sin atone,
Lord, shall I flee?

Thy wounds, not mine, O Christ,
Can heal my bruised soul;
Thy stripes, not mine, contain
The balm that makes me whole. *(Refrain)*

Thy cross, not mine, O Christ,
Has borne the crushing load
Of sins that none could bear
But the incarnate God. *(Refrain)*

Thy death, not mine, O Christ,
Has paid the ransom due;
Ten thousand deaths like mine
Would have been all too few. *(Refrain)*

Thy righteousness, O Christ,
Alone can cover me;
No righteousness avails
Save that which is of Thee. *(Refrain)*
(*LSB* 565:1–5)

Lamentation

LAMENTATION

Luke 23:50–56

This illustration depicts the intense shock and mourning that followed the crucifixion as Nicodemus completes his descent from the cross with the body of Christ. Although the women of Galilee were obscure in the previous print, Dürer now portrays them in animated grief. These are some of the same women who, according to Luke, "had been healed of evil spirits and infirmities," traveled with Jesus, and financially supported His ministry (Luke 8:2). They thought they understood the life-giving forgiveness of sins in His preaching and miracles. And now their Lord was dead! One woman raises her hands and voice in loud lament. Mary Magdalene, "from whom seven demons had gone out" kisses His nail-pierced feet (Luke 8:2).

Mary, the mother of Jesus, feels the sharp pain of Simeon's prophecy to the very depths of her soul. Unable to stand, she is supported by the disciple John. The hands that held the newborn Christ now reach to touch His lifeless body. Behind the cross, Joseph of Arimathea is waiting with burial spices and linens. Nicodemus, a secret follower who had come to speak with Jesus under the cover of night, now holds the fulfillment of the Rabbi's words in his arms. "For God so loved the world, that He gave His only Son, that whoever believes in Him should not perish but have eternal life" (John 3:16).

> Joseph of Arimathea, who was a disciple of Jesus,
> but secretly for fear of the Jews, asked Pilate that
> he might take away the body of Jesus, and Pilate
> gave him permission. So he came and took away
> His body. Nicodemus also, who earlier had come to
> Jesus by night, came bringing a mixture of myrrh
> and aloes, about seventy-five pounds in weight. So
> they took the body of Jesus and bound it in linen
> cloths with the spices, as is the burial custom of
> the Jews. (John 19:38–40)

It is 3 o'clock on Friday afternoon, the Day of
Preparation for the Sabbath. According to Jewish law,
the burial must be completed before sundown. Who will
bury Jesus? Other than John, His closest companions have
already fled in fear of their lives, and remain in hiding.
But two secret disciples, members of the Sanhedrin, have
emerged from fear and hiding. What courage it must have
taken for Joseph of Arimathea to ask Pilate for the body of
Jesus! Usually, crucified criminals were given a pauper's
burial.

Hasty preparations are made. Shroud linens are
purchased. Nicodemus brings seventy-five pounds of spices
and embalming oils, assuming the body will decay. For
Jesus is dead. The women lament. The spear thrust into the
heart of Christ by the Roman soldier leaves no doubt as to
this fact: Jesus Christ, the Son of God, is dead. Why is it so
important that His death is real? Without death, there can
be no resurrection. Without death, there can be no payment
for sin. The death of Christ is the certainty that our sins are
forgiven. The blood from His side cleanses us from sin. We
are made clean in the blood of the Lamb. By His death we

are set free from eternal death. "But God shows His love for us in that while we were still sinners, Christ died for us. Since, therefore, we have been justified by His blood, much more shall we be saved by Him from the wrath of God" (Romans 5:8–9).

> Alas! And did my Savior bleed,
>   And did my sov'reign die?
> Would He devote that sacred head
>   For such a worm as I?
>
> Was it for crimes that I had done
>   He groaned upon the tree?
> Amazing pity, grace unknown,
>   And love beyond degree!
>
> Well might the sun in darkness hide
>   And shut his glories in
> When God, the mighty maker, died
>   For His own creatures' sin.
>
> Thus might I hide my blushing face
>   While His dear cross appears,
> Dissolve my heart in thankfulness,
>   And melt mine eyes to tears.
>
> But drops of grief can ne'er repay
>   The debt of love I owe;
> Here, Lord, I give myself away:
>   'Tis all that I can do.
>
>   (*LSB* 437:1–5)

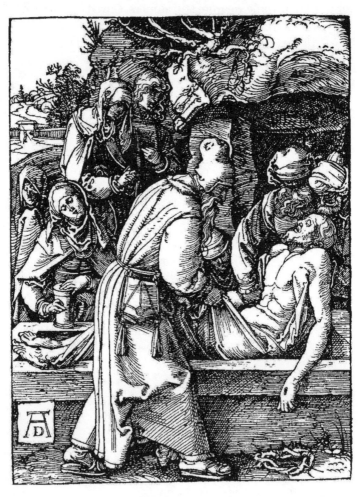

Entombment

THE ENTOMBMENT

Matthew 27:57–61

Renaissance artwork often portrays the burial of Christ in an outdoor setting with the sepulcher pictured in the background. Dürer makes use of this technique to create room for the viewer in such an intimate scene. The pierced hand and crown seem close enough to touch. One can almost feel the coldness of death and the stab of the thorn. Even the artist's presence makes itself known. His monogram stands out in stark white against the gray stone sarcophagus, identifying his own sin with the death of Christ. The tentacles of Eden's tree of death cling to the entrance of the rocky tomb.

Wringing her hands in grief, Mary, the mother of Jesus, stands close to John. Mary Magdalene waits with an anointing jar. She and another Galilean woman, unable to bear the sight, wait with eyes downcast. Joseph of Arimathea and Nicodemus gently lower the body of Jesus into the tomb originally meant to be Joseph's own death chamber. The scene is sad, pitiful, and hopeless. Hadn't they recently been at another tomb? Hadn't they witnessed Jesus' command to Lazarus, and seen a man four days dead come out of his grave? How can the Lord of life be dead?

> Then Jesus, deeply moved again, came to the tomb.
> . . . He cried out with a loud voice, "Lazarus, come
> out." The man who had died came out, his hands
> and feet bound with linen strips, and his face
> wrapped with a cloth. Jesus said to them, "Unbind
> him, and let him go." (John 11:38, 43–44)

Mere weeks earlier, Jesus and His followers had been at another grave. Jesus had wept at the tomb of Lazarus. Even though Christ knew He would raise His friend from the dead in just a few minutes, His heart grieved at the sight and smell of death. Death brings tears, and the Lord of life cried. When we stand at the graveside of loved ones, our Savior feels our pain of separation. This is the terrible separation that began in the Garden of Eden. It is the separation between God and Adam, which brought the curse of death into the life of all mankind. This is why Jesus came. He is the perfect Second Adam. He came to live our life. He came to die our death. He came to lie in our tomb. Lazarus, too, was dead. The decomposition process had already begun. Yet the word of the Lord brings life! "Unbind him and let him go!" Just as the word of new creation released Lazarus from death's prison, it promises our release from the prison of eternal death. Jesus proclaims, "I am the resurrection and the life. Whoever believes in Me, though he die, yet shall he live" (John 11:25).

Now Jesus is given a traditional Jewish burial. His friends anoint His body with oils, binding His corpse with strips of linen, embalming spices tucked into the folds of the fabric. They wrap His face in a cloth, and He is placed into a new tomb. But new life will spring from this tomb— new life for all believers in Christ. Our Savior's rest in the tomb hallows the graves of all Christians as we wait for the resurrection of the dead. We wait for the voice of Jesusto us: "Unbind him and let him go!"

O darkest woe!
Ye tears, forth flow!
     Has earth so sad a
     wonder?
God the Father's only Son
     Now is buried yonder.

O sorrow dread!
God's Son is dead!
     But by His expiation
Of our guilt upon the cross
     Gained for us salvation.

O sinful man!
It was the ban
     Of death on thee that
     brought Him
Down to suffer for thy sins
     And such woe hath
     wrought Him.

Lo, stained with blood,
The Lamb of God,
     The Bridegroom, lies
     before thee,
Pouring out His life that He
     May to life restore thee.

O Ground of faith,
Laid low in death,
     Sweet lips, now silent
     sleeping!
Surely all that lives must mourn
     Here with bitter weeping.

O blest shall be
Eternally
     Who oft in faith will
     ponder
Why the glorious Prince of Life
     Should be buried yonder.

O Jesus blest,
My Help and Rest,
     With tears I now entreat
     Thee:
Make me love Thee to the last,
     Till in heaven I greet Thee.
          (*TLH* 167:1–7)

Resurrection

THE RESURRECTION

Matthew 28:1–10

The image of the living and triumphant Christ dominates the Easter woodcut. The artist pictures the exact moment of the resurrection. In the foreground the stunned guards are knocked to the ground. They shield their eyes from the dazzling glory of the resurrected Christ, "and for fear of Him the guards trembled and became like dead men" (Matthew 28:4).

In the distance the women can be seen coming to the tomb as the first rays of sunshine penetrate the gloom of night. Mount Calvary, topped with a tree reminiscent of the Garden of Eden and Adam's sin, is in the background. Shroud linens have become the King's mantle. His scepter and resurrection banner proclaim the victory of the cross. The large white cloud is similar to the one in Dürer's *Annunciation* print. It symbolizes the presence of God the Father. It shows His approval of the perfect sacrifice of His Son, the Second Adam, for the sins of all mankind. The deity of Christ is clearly shown by the Trinitarian nimbus. His body, with wounds of side, feet, and hands, proclaims His humanity. "It is finished!" (John 19:30). Death is defeated. Christ is risen! He is risen indeed! Alleluia!

And behold, Jesus met them and said, "Greetings!"
And they came up and took hold of His feet and
worshiped Him. Then Jesus said to them, "Do not
be afraid; go and tell My brothers to go to Galilee,
and there they will see Me." (Matthew 28:9–10)

"Do not be afraid." What wonderful words! This is the
angel's Christmas song at the birth of Christ. This is the
angel's Easter hymn at the empty tomb of Christ. These are
the first recorded words of the risen Christ as He speaks
comfort to fearful women, and to you and me. These faithful
followers of Jesus had left their homes in the early morning,
in the darkness of sorrow and despair. They had come in
tears to anoint their Lord's dead body. They had come with
broken hearts. The angel's words were astonishing. Running
from the open tomb, the women are greeted by the Lord of
life. "Do not be afraid; go and tell my brothers."

Good news! This is what all creation had been waiting
for. Death's reign is over! Sins are forgiven! Salvation is
accomplished! The resurrection is the Father's glorious
amen to the sacrifice of His Son on Calvary's cross. God
declares that all sins have been forgiven by the death of
Christ. Perfect payment has been made for the guilt of all
mankind. It is God's free gift to us. In the death of Christ
we are justified. We are declared innocent. The broken
relationship between the Creator and His creation is healed.
The curse of death brought by Adam's sin is destroyed.
Death is no longer our prison. Through faith in the atoning
sacrifice of Christ, heaven is opened to all believers. In the
resurrection of the Passover Lamb, we pass with Him from
death to life!

Christ Jesus lay in death's strong bands
　　For our offenses given;
But now at God's right hand He stands
　　And brings us life from heaven.
Therefore let us joyful be
And sing to God right thankfully
　　Loud songs of alleluia! Alleluia!

No son of man could conquer death,
　　Such ruin sin had wrought us,
No innocence was found on earth,
　　And therefore death had brought us
Into bondage from of old
And ever grew more strong and bold
　　And held us as its captive. ~~Alleluia!~~

Christ Jesus, God's own Son, came down,
　　His people to deliver;
Destroying sin, He took the crown
　　From death's pale brow forever:
Stripped of pow'r, no more it reigns;
An empty form alone remains;
　　Its sting is lost forever. Alleluia!

Here our true Paschal Lamb we see,
　　Whom God so freely gave us;
He died on the accursed tree—
　　So strong His love—to save us.
See, His blood now marks our door;
Faith points to it; death passes o'er,
　　And Satan cannot harm us. Alleluia!
　　　　　　(*LSB* 458:1–3, 5)

Noli Me Tangere

Noli Me Tangere

John 20:11–18

This charming print is probably the most recognized and loved out of all of the woodcuts in Albrecht Dürer's *Small Passion*. It is early on Easter morning. The sun's first rays illuminate the risen Lord as Mary Magdalene kneels before Him. Dressed as a gardener, Christ's resurrection ushers in His new creation. He holds a shovel over His shoulder; the work is done. The sin in the Garden of Eden has been paid for on the cross by the Second Adam. He is the obedient, perfect gardener.

Although the title, *Noli Me Tangere,* Latin for "Do Not Touch Me," has been used for many paintings in the Renaissance period, it is, unfortunately, a poor translation. Rather, Jesus gives Mary Magdalene two urgent imperatives. First, she is to stop clinging and holding on to Him. Second, she is to journey to His disciples and tell them the Good News. He has risen! He has defeated sin, death, and Satan. The relationship destroyed in the Garden of Eden between God and man is now restored. "They shall call His name Immanuel (which means, God with us)" (Matthew 1:23). The promise of a Savior in Genesis 3:15 has been fulfilled. "Go to My brothers and say to them, 'I am ascending to My Father and your Father, to My God and your God' " (John 20:17). In the crucified and risen Christ, we are made children of the heavenly Father!

> But Mary stood weeping outside the tomb, and
> as she wept she stooped to look into the tomb.
> And she saw two angels in white, sitting where the
> body of Jesus had lain, one at the head and one at
> the feet. They said to her, "Woman, why are you
> weeping?" (John 20:11–13a)

All of the followers of Jesus begin Easter morning with heavy, fearful hearts. None of them remember their Lord's many predictions. Jesus had plainly taught them that He "must suffer many things and be rejected by the elders and the chief priests and the scribes and be killed, and after three days rise again" (Mark 8:31). But most of them were in hiding. Only a few ventured to the tomb. Mary Magdalene was also a faithful follower of Jesus. She loved her Lord and stayed with Him to the end. She stood at the cross. She saw Him die. She watched His body laid into the grave. Now she is overcome with weeping at the empty tomb. Her tears blind her to the important truth of the angels' presence. So deep is her sorrow that she does not even recognize Jesus.

How often are we like Mary Magdalene? When sorrow and troubles enter our lives, do we recognize the living voice of Christ in His Word? Do our tears blind us to His constant loving presence in our lives? Do we forget that we are bound to the resurrected Lord through His body and blood? Do we cling to our Baptism when God put His name on us, marking us with the sign of the cross? Do we remember God's promise to use all things for good, just as He used the suffering and death of Christ for our good? On our own we cannot seek Jesus, so our Good Shepherd calls us by name, as He did for Mary at the empty tomb. In His Holy Word He calls us His brothers. He assures us that, through His death, God has forgiven our sins. What great comfort that we can call God, the Creator of all things, our Father! In the resurrection of Christ, we are assured that we, too, will rise from the dead and ascend to His Father and to our Father. This is the joy of Easter, which gives peace to the most fearful of hearts.

Awake, my heart with gladness, / See what today is done; / Now, after gloom and sadness, / Comes forth the glorious sun. / My Savior there was laid / Where our bed must be made / When to the realms of light / Our spirit wings its flight.

The foe in triumph shouted / When Christ lay in the tomb; / But lo, he now is routed, / His boast is turned to gloom. / For Christ again is free; / In glorious victory / He who is strong to save / Has triumphed o'er the grave.

This is a sight that gladdens— / What peace it doth impart! / Now nothing ever saddens / The joy within my heart. / No gloom shall ever shake, / No foe shall ever take / The hope which God's own Son In love for me has won.

Now I will cling forever / To Christ, my Savior true; / My Lord will leave me never, / Whate'er He passes through. / He rends death's iron chain; / He breaks through sin and pain; / He shatters hell's grim thrall; / I follow Him through all.

He brings me to the portal / That leads to bliss untold, / Whereon this rhyme immortal / Is found in script of gold: / "Who there My cross has shared / Finds here a crown prepared; / Who there with Me has died / Shall here be glorified."

(*LSB* 467:1–3, 6–7)

Supper at Emmaus

SUPPER AT EMMAUS

Luke 24:13–35

The Emmaus woodcut captures the stunning moment of faith's recognition of the Savior. Jesus, is the host at the meal. His presence brings forgiveness, life, and salvation. These gifts were destroyed at the first meal in the Garden of Eden. Just as the nail-pierced hands of Jesus are breaking the bread, the eyes of Cleopas, dressed as a Renaissance traveler, are opened. He clutches his heart. It is the Lord! The risen Lord! Suddenly, all the truths of Scripture their traveling companion had taught them on the afternoon's walk become crystal clear. Although the Lukan narrative mentions only two people, the artist has inserted several others in the background, providing a foretaste of the Holy Christian Church, where many will gather in the real presence of Christ. Dürer leaves space at the end of the small table for you to join in the supper. He also is present, for his monogram is on the bench, as well as in the table legs and cloth.

Cleopas will return to Jerusalem, not in doubt and sorrow as before, but in faith and joy, proclaiming the Good News. All Jesus had said is true! "See, we are going up to Jerusalem, and everything that is written about the Son of Man by the prophets will be accomplished. For He will be delivered over to the Gentiles and will be mocked and shamefully treated and spit upon. And after flogging Him, they will kill Him, and on the third day He will rise" (Luke 18:31–33). He lives! On the first day of the new creation, the room at Emmaus is filled with the radiance of the large, glorious, cross-shaped nimbus around the resurrected Lord.

And He said to them, "O foolish ones, and slow of
heart to believe all that the prophets have spoken!
Was it not necessary that the Christ should
suffer these things and enter into His glory?" And
beginning with Moses and all the Prophets, He
interpreted to them in all the Scriptures the things
concerning Himself. (Luke 24:25–27)

It is late afternoon of Easter, but for the disciples there is
no joy, their hearts still heavy with grief. No one believes the
women's account of the angels' message at the empty tomb.
While the eleven remain hidden, two disciples from the
larger group of seventy journey the seven miles to the town
of Emmaus. Jesus meets them on the road! Keeping His
identity hidden, He questions them about their sadness. He
gives them the opportunity to unburden their heavy hearts,
and Cleopas tells the sad story. Their hope for the freedom of
Israel was crushed in the death of a mighty prophet. Instead
of revealing Himself to them as the risen Christ, Jesus points
them to Scripture. He teaches them to see the crucified and
risen Christ as the fulfillment of the entire Old Testament.
He shows them that God's promise to rescue His people was
not an earthly political freedom, but an eternal spiritual
freedom from the bondage of sin and death. Slowly, their
hearts begin to burn with faith. Arriving at their destination
they beg Jesus, "Stay with us" (Luke 24:28). A meal is served.
Jesus speaks the blessing. He breaks the bread, "and their
eyes were opened, and they recognized Him" (Luke 24:31).

As we journey the road of life, we too are slow of heart.
On our own we cannot know Jesus. Today, nearly two
thousand years later, the risen Christ still teaches us in
the same manner. In the Divine Service He comes with the

forgiveness of sins in His Word and in the breaking of bread. Eyes are opened! Faith rejoices in the risen Savior. Stay with us, O Lord.

Who are you who walk in sorrow
Down Emmaus' barren road,
Hearts distraught and hope defeated,
Bent beneath grief's crushing load?
Nameless mourners, we will join you,
We who also mourn our dead;
We have stood by graves unyielding,
Eaten death's bare, bitter bread.

Who is this who joins our journey,
Walking with us stride by stride?
Unknown Stranger, can you fathom
Depths of grief for one who died?
Then the wonder! When we told You
How our dreams to dust have turned,
Then you opened wide the Scriptures
Till our hearts within us burned.

Who are You? Our hearts are opened
In the breaking of the bread—
Christ the victim, now the victor
Living, risen from the dead!
Great companion on our journey,
Still surprise us with Your grace!
Make each day a new Emmaus;
On our hearts Your image trace!
(*LSB* 476:1–3)

Christ Appearing to His Disciples

CHRIST APPEARING TO HIS DISCIPLES

John 20:24–29

All eleven disciples are present in Dürer's pictorial account of the second Sunday of Easter, the eighth day of the new creation. Jesus, wearing a mantle of victory, is large and central. He raises His hand in blessing, dispelling all fear and apprehension. His presence brings light to the darkness of the locked room and the locked heart of His doubting disciple.

The Savior's gaze is gentle and loving as it focuses on Thomas. Rather than abandoning him to unbelief, Jesus patiently complies with Thomas's conditions. He gives opportunity for weak faith to grow strong. The artist depicts the poignant scene as Jesus firmly grasps the hand of Thomas, placing it into His wounded side. Nothing is hidden. Not only can Thomas see the five wounds of Christ, but by invitation he can feel the warm, vibrant flesh, and the blood and bone of the Lord of Life. Faith responds with confession in the incarnate Son of God! This is the apostolic confession of the Holy Christian Church as it gathers around the living voice of Christ and His body and blood: "And in Jesus Christ, His only Son our Lord . . . "

Eight days later, His disciples were inside again, and Thomas was with them. Although the doors were locked, Jesus came and stood among them and said, "Peace be with you." Then He said to Thomas, "Put your finger here, and see My hands; and put out your hand, and place it in My side. Do not disbelieve, but believe." Thomas answered Him, "My Lord and My God!" (John 20:26–28)

Thomas is no different than the other disciples. He is just a week behind the rest, having been absent when Jesus appeared to the other ten on Easter evening. Thomas did not believe their words. This is the same stunning report that Mary Magdalene and the other women gave to the disciples on Easter morning. They did not believe either. They were not convinced until the risen Christ miraculously appeared to them. And we are no different. It is easy to believe in Jesus when life is rosy and sweet. But when the murky darkness of adversity enters our lives, we also doubt God's presence. Satan tempts us to abandon our Savior. Faith turns to doubt.

But Jesus comes to us, not with condemnation for unbelief, but with the good news of the Gospel: "Peace be with you" (John 20:19). The Redeemer of the world comes with the peace of the forgiveness of sins. This is the song of the Christmas angels. "Glory to God in the highest, and on earth peace among those with whom He is pleased!" (Luke

2:14). The very wounds of battle that Thomas touches are the very wounds that brought victory over death, and salvation for all who believe. This very same body of the risen and crucified Lord still comes to us today with the forgiveness of sin in His Supper of Holy Communion. He comes with the words "Peace be with you." God and mankind are united in the victory of the incarnate Christ. Together with Thomas, faith responds, "My Lord and my God!" (John 20:28).

When Thomas first the tidings heard
That they had seen the risen Lord,
He doubted the disciples' word.
 Alleluia!

"My pierced side, O Thomas, see,
And look upon My hands, My feet;
Not faithless but believing be."
 Alleluia!

No longer Thomas then denied;
He saw the feet, the hands, the side;
"You are my Lord and God!" he cried.
 Alleluia!

How blest are they who have not seen
And yet whose faith has constant been,
For they eternal life shall win.
 Alleluia!

(*LSB* 471:5–8)

Ascension

The Ascension

Acts 1:6–12

Forty days after Easter, Jesus has gathered the eleven disciples on the Mount of Olives for His last appearance. Their expressions convey awe and amazement as they worship their departing Savior. At first glance this woodcut may seem silly or even absurd. But Dürer has given the viewer the profound opportunity to witness the biblical truth, confessed in the Apostles' Creed: "He ascended into heaven." It is as if you are present for the exact historical moment at which the crucified and risen Lord departs from earth to return to reign with His heavenly Father. Looking up, the disciples see Christ already enveloped in the clouds, His feet and trailing garments still visible in the last second of our Lord's earthly ministry.

Although the footprints embedded in the rock are merely legend, they illustrate the truth of the incarnation. God became Man and lived on earth in the blood, bones, flesh, and feet of Jesus Christ. The footprints also serve as a reminder of His promise to remain with all believers until His second coming: "Behold, I am with you always, to the end of the age" (Matthew 28:20b).

The hooded female figure is Mary. She is symbolic of the Holy Christian Church, who waits in expectation for her Lord's return.

Then He led them out as far as Bethany, and lifting up His hands He blessed them. While He blessed them, He parted from them and was carried up into heaven. And they worshiped Him and returned to Jerusalem with great joy, and were continually in the temple blessing God. (Luke 24:50–53)

Jesus' earthly work is done. He came from heaven in great humility as a tiny, helpless baby, to live a life of suffering and death in payment for our sin and guilt. Now He returns to His Father in majesty and triumph as the victorious, living Christ. Our Lord has accomplished all He was sent to do as our perfect substitute. Sin, death, and Satan are defeated in His crucifixion and resurrection. This work was not for His own benefit, but for us. Jesus ascends as true man and true God for us. He returns to heaven in flesh, to be our brother and to reign with God the Father. As He departs, Jesus lifts His hands in blessing. The same hands that were nailed to the cross in shame and weakness now bestow blessings of promise and peace.

What does it mean to be blessed? It is not earthly happiness, but the eternal showering of God's favor. All that is Christ's is now ours. His ascension gives the promise of our ascension. "And if I go and prepare a place for you, I will come again and will take you to Myself, that where I am you may be also" (John 14:3). Although Jesus visibly leaves the earth, He promises to be with us by His Spirit, in His Word and Sacraments. He gives His Church pastors to continue the apostles' work, to proclaim repentance and forgiveness in the name of Christ, and to lift their hands in blessing, bestowing upon His people the peace of God.

With the disciples we respond with great joy, continually blessing our ascended Lord for His life-giving presence among us.

> On Christ's ascension I now build
> The hope of my ascension;
> This hope alone has always stilled
> All doubt and apprehension;
> For where the Head is, there as well
> I know His members are to dwell
> When Christ shall come and call them.
>
> Since Christ returned to claim His throne,
> Great gifts for me obtaining,
> My heart will rest in Him alone,
> No other rest remaining;
> For where my treasure went before,
> There all my thoughts will ever soar
> To still their deepest yearning.
>
> O grant, dear Lord, this grace to me,
> Recalling Your ascension,
> That I may serve You faithfully
> In thanks for my redemption;
> And then, when all my days will cease,
> Let me depart in joy and peace
> In answer to my pleading.
> (*LSB* 492)

Descent of the Holy Spirit

DESCENT OF THE HOLY SPIRIT

Acts 2:1–13

Dürer's woodcut of the Pentecost account centers on the coming of the Holy Spirit to the apostles. It is ten days after Christ's ascension into heaven. The third person of the Holy Trinity is depicted as a dove as divine rays emanate in all directions. They fill not only the room with God's presence, but the very fiber of the disciples themselves. Tongues of fire rest on their heads. Glowing with the gift of the Holy Spirit, the disciples display awe and adoration. They proclaim the Gospel of the crucified, risen, and ascended Lord in the tongues of many languages.

Three figures stand out in the foreground. Peter stands boldly on the right, his hands spread in wonder. He is the great spokesman of the apostles, and he preaches the first sermon on the birthday of the Holy Christian Church. John stands in the left corner, and in the center of the print, the third figure, Mary the mother of Jesus, holds a book. Although the biblical account of Pentecost does not mention her specifically, it is likely that she was present since she and the other women stayed in the Upper Room with the disciples after the ascension, as recorded in Acts 1:12–14. Here Mary symbolizes the Church. While she waits for Christ's return, she cradles the Word of God, as she had cradled the Word made flesh at His first coming.

"Let all the house of Israel therefore know for certain that God has made Him both Lord and Christ, this Jesus whom you crucified." Now when they heard this they were cut to the heart, and said to Peter and the rest of the apostles, "Brothers, what shall we do?" And Peter said to them, "Repent and be baptized every one of you in the name of Jesus Christ for the forgiveness of your sins, and you will receive the gift of the Holy Spirit." (Acts 2:36–38)

Peter's sermon on Pentecost is a magnificent proclamation of Law and Gospel. By the power of the Holy Spirit, fearful disciples hidden behind locked doors become eloquent, public preachers to thousands of religious pilgrims from many countries. The rushing wind and tongues of fire transform ordinary fishermen into theologians. They confidently speak in languages they have never learned. Peter, blunt in his boldness, convicts the crowd of killing the promised Messiah, the Son of God. But this sermon is not just for people in Jerusalem two thousand years ago. It applies to us today. We, too, are guilty. The sin of Adam clings to us. We are all born in sin and continue to deny our God and our neighbors in our thoughts, words, and deeds. We deserve the wrath of God just as intensely as the Jewish leaders who rejected Christ, and the Roman soldiers who nailed Him to the cross. It is our sin that crucified the Son of God. Fearful hearts cry out in terror of eternal damnation! What shall we do?

Repent—confess your sins. "Have mercy on me, O God; according to Your steadfast love; according to Your abundant mercy blot out my transgressions" (Psalm 51:1).

Be baptized—washed in the waters of forgiveness of sins. "Baptism . . . now saves you, not as a removal of dirt from the body but as an appeal to God for a good conscience, through the resurrection of Jesus Christ" (1 Peter 3:21). In Baptism we are given the gift of the Holy Spirit. It is the gift of faith in Christ Jesus our Savior.

> Come, Holy Ghost, God and Lord,
> With all Your graces now outpoured
> On each believer's mind and heart;
> Your fervent love to them impart.
> Lord, by the brightness of Your light
> In holy faith Your Church unite;
> From ev'ry land and ev'ry tongue
> This to Your praise, O Lord, Our God, be sung:
> Alleluia, alleluia!
>
> Come, holy Light, guide divine,
> Now cause the Word of life to shine.
> Teach us to know our God aright
> And call Him Father with delight.
> From ev'ry error keep us free;
> Let none but Christ our master be
> That we in living faith abide,
> In Him, our Lord, with all our might confide.
> Alleluia, alleluia!
>
> Come, Holy Fire, comfort true,
> Grant us the will Your work to do
> And in Your service to abide;
> Let trials turn us not aside.
> Lord, by Your pow'r prepare each heart,
> And to our weakness strength impart
> That bravely here we may contend,
> Through life and death to You, our Lord, ascend.
> Alleluia, alleluia!
>
> (*LSB* 497)

Last Judgment

THE LAST JUDGMENT

Matthew 25:31–46

he final print reflects the confession of the Nicene Creed: "And He will come again with glory to judge both the living and the dead." With the wounds of His Passion visible, the image of Jesus is radiant. The exalted Lord descends in clouds of heavenly glory, surrounded by trumpeting angels who herald His coming. The nimbus reflects divine power and authority. The Lord of Creation rests His feet on the earth's orb as the dead beneath Him rise from their graves. Mary, the mother of Jesus, and John the Baptist, the last prophet, kneel in worship. These two saints represent the entirety of the Holy Christian Church.

The judgment has begun. Christ declares the believers justified, His hand pointing upward and the lily, icon of purity, projecting from His head. They are innocent of all sin by His death on the cross. On His left, the sword and the palm turned downward pronounce the condemnation of those who reject Christ's atonement for their sin. This fulfillment of the Genesis curse and promise is depicted in the foreground. In one corner, devilish creatures mercilessly push chained unbelievers into the mouth of hell's dragon. On the other side, saints are ushered into heaven's glory by angels, reversing man's exile from Eden.

This final woodcut in Dürer's *Small Passion* is the confession of the Te Deum (We Praise You, O God): "We believe that You will come to be our judge. We therefore pray You to help Your servants, whom You have redeemed with Your precious blood. Make them to be numbered with Your saints in glory everlasting" (*LSB*, pp. 224–25).

> Then the King will say to those on His right, "Come, you who are blessed by My Father, inherit the kingdom prepared for you from the foundation of the world. For I was hungry and you gave Me food, I was thirsty and you gave Me drink, I was a stranger and you welcomed Me" . . . then the righteous will answer Him saying, "Lord when did we see You hungry and feed You, or thirsty and give You drink?" . . . and the King will answer them, "Truly, I say to you, as you did it to one of the least of these My brothers, you did it to Me." (Matthew 25:34–35, 37, 40)

Though no one knows when the world will end, Jesus explains precisely how the events of the Last Day will unfold. While the day is not known, the events themselves are not hidden. His first coming to earth was in meekness and lowliness, to suffer and die for our sins. Having accomplished salvation by His death on the cross, the second coming will be in power and majesty. Christ will come to judge all people, living and dead. He will judge men's hearts. His verdict for each person will mean eternal life or eternal death. For the unbeliever, this will be the fulfillment of the Law. All those who reject Jesus' sacrifice as the complete payment for all their sins will be declared guilty before the Almighty God. They will be cast "into the eternal fire prepared for the devil and his angels" (Matthew 25:41).

But for believers, Judgment Day will be the fulfillment of the Gospel. We have already been judged and found innocent by the death of Christ. Having been already justified, we are free to live the Christian life in service to others. Our sins no longer count against us, and our good works are not tallied to earn salvation. Sinners could never do enough kind deeds to appease the wrath of God, so Jesus did the good work for us on Calvary's cross. Salvation is a completely free gift from God. Loving our neighbor is the joyful response that naturally flows from the Christian heart in thanksgiving. Praise God! We are saved by grace alone, through faith in Christ Jesus. Not our works, but His work alone opens heaven to all believers. "Amen. Come, Lord Jesus!" (Revelation 22:20).

> The day is surely drawing near
>   When Jesus, God's anointed,
> In all His power shall appear
>   As judge whom God appointed.
> Then fright shall banish idle mirth,
> And flames on flames shall ravish earth
>   As Scripture long has warned us.
>
> The final trumpet then shall sound
>   And all the earth be shaken,
> And all who rest beneath the ground
>   Shall from their sleep awaken.
> But all who live will in that hour,
> By God's almighty, boundless pow'r,
>   Be changed at His commanding.

The books are opened then to all,
    A record truly telling
What each has done both great and small,
    When he on earth was dwelling,
And ev'ry heart be clearly seen,
And all be known as they have been
    In thoughts and words and actions.

Then woe to those who scorned the Lord
    And sought but carnal pleasures,
Who here despised His precious Word
    And loved their earthly treasures!
With shame and trembling they will stand
And at the judge's stern command
    To Satan be delivered.

My Savior paid the debt I owe
    And for my sin was smitten;
Within the Book of Life I know
    My name has now been written.
I will not doubt, for I am free,
And Satan cannot threaten me;
    There is no condemnation!

May Christ our intercessor be
    And through His blood and merit
Read from His book that we are free
    With all who life inherit.
Then we shall see Him face to face,
With all His saints in that blest place
    Which He has purchased for us.
        (*LSB* 508:1–6)

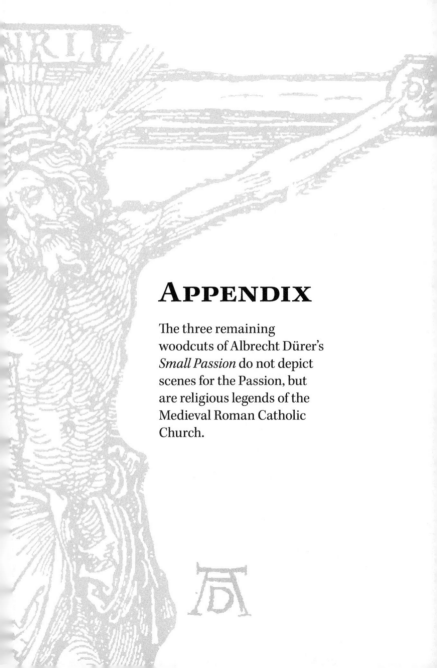

Appendix

The three remaining
woodcuts of Albrecht Dürer's
Small Passion do not depict
scenes for the Passion, but
are religious legends of the
Medieval Roman Catholic
Church.

Sudarium

Sudarium

udarium is the Latin word for a handkerchief, used to wipe sweat. Legend states that a woman named Veronica wiped the face of Christ as He carried His cross on the road to Calvary. The cloth is said to miraculously bear the imprint of His face and the crown of thorns. Although the original is reported to have been lost, an indistinguishable duplicate is enshrined as a relic in a chapel at St. Peter's Basilica, Rome.

Dürer pictures Veronica holding the Sudarium between St. Peter and St. Paul.

Christ in Limbo

CHRIST IN LIMBO

This woodcut illustrates the Medieval Roman Catholic Church's legend of Christ descending into Limbo between the time of His death and resurrection. Limbo is said to be a cavern on the edge of hell where the faithful Old Testament saints were kept until the death of Christ. The artist shows Jesus, having torn the gate from the dungeon, rescuing Abraham. Previously freed, Adam, Eve, and John the Baptist are surrounded by devilish creatures. Two crosses are seen. Calvary's cross looms in the background while the resurrection banner and cross are carried by Jesus.

Both the Apostles' Creed and the Athanasian Creed confess that Christ "descended into hell" after His crucifixion at the time of the resurrection. This was not to suffer more punishment for the sin of mankind. The full payment had been made for sin on the cross. Rather, as is recorded in 1 Peter 3:18–19, the risen Christ journeyed to hell to proclaim His victory over sin, death, and Satan. The "spirits in prison" were not God's faithful believers, but those who had rejected His grace and were condemned. Various accounts of Scripture testify that believers who died before the death of Christ were justified and given the gifts of forgiveness, life, and salvation. Hebrews chapter 11 records that the Old Testament saints were saved by their faith in the promised Savior. Furthermore, in the Transfiguration accounts, a glimpse of heaven is seen. Luke 9:28–36 states that Moses and Elijah appeared with Jesus in heavenly glory as they discussed His coming suffering, crucifixion, resurrection, and ascension.

Christ Appearing to His Mother

CHRIST APPEARING TO HIS MOTHER

N one of the Gospel accounts of the resurrection record an intimate meeting of Jesus and His mother, Mary after the resurrection. This legend first occurred in writing in the fourth century by St. Ambrose. Specific details were later fleshed out by Pseudo-Bonaventura around 1300. The legend became official Roman Catholic doctrine at the Council of Trent, which met from 1545–1563.

The woodcut shows a kneeling Mary reading Scripture, similar to the *Annunciation*.

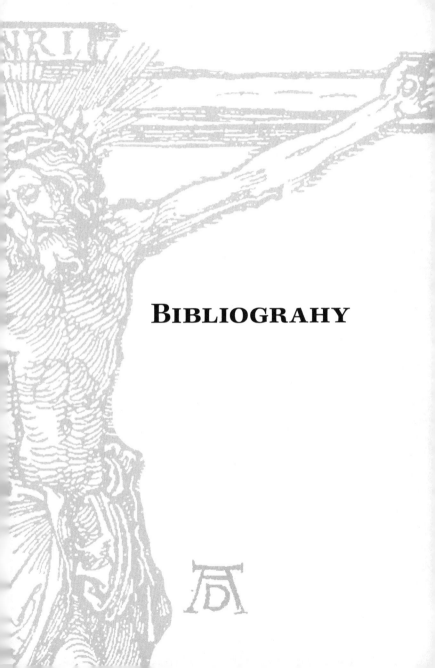

BIBLIOGRAHY

Bibliography

Anzelewsky, Fedja. *Dürer: His Art and Life.* Translated by Heide Grieve. New York: Publishers of Fine Books, 1980.

Bartrum, Giulia. *Albrecht Dürer and His Legacy.* London: The British Museum Press, 2002.

Conway, William Martin, trans. and ed. *The Writings of Albrecht Dürer.* New York: Philosophical Library, 1958.

Ferguson, George. *Signs and Symbols in Christian Art.* New York: Oxford University Press, 1961.

Hall, James. *Dictionary of Subjects and Symbols in Art.* London: John Murray, 1996.

Hutchison, Jane Campbell. *Albrecht Dürer: A Biography.* Princeton: Princeton University Press 1990.

Kantor, Jordan. *Dürer's Passions.* Cambridge, MA: Harvard University Art Museum, 2000.

Metford, J. C. J. *Dictionary of Christian Lore and Legend*. London: Thames and Hudson, 1983.

Panofsky, Erwin. *Albrecht Dürer*. Vol. 1. Princeton: Princeton University Press, 1948.

Russell, Francis. *The World of Dürer: 1471–1528*. New York: Time Incorporated, 1967.

Spitz, Lewis W. *The Renaissance and Reformation Movements*. St. Louis: Concordia, 1971.

Strauss, Walter L., ed. *The Complete Engravings, Etchings, And Drypoints of Albrecht Dürer*. New York: Dover Publications, Inc., 1973.

Wölfflin, Heinrich. *The Art of Albrecht Dürer*. Translated by Alastair and Heide Grieve. London: Phaidon Press Limited, 1971.